Praise for Lewis R[...]
A Whole Life'[...]

"In a playful and pleasant voice, Lewis Richmond ennobles all the works of our lives and erases the idea that spiritual practice requires 'time off.' Who would have thought that reading a book about work could be delightful as well as such good dharma?"

—Sylvia Boorstein,
author of *Pay Attention, for Goodness' Sake:
Practicing the Perfections of the Heart—
The Buddhist Path of Kindness*

"Richmond skillfully blends example, Buddhist precept, inquiry, and anecdote in each chapter, and the result is a provocative and profound meditation on a part of life as inescapable as death and taxes. Highly recommended."

—*Library Journal*

"[This] wonderful book may be the first truly American book of Buddhist practice. If it's not the first, it is certainly among the most memorable. . . . It will inspire your gratitude for its existence. It will change you."

—Peter Coyote, actor and author of *Sleeping Where I Fall*

"Richmond uses the remarkable awareness of a highly trained Zen practitioner to give us an intimate account of a confrontation with disease, disability, near-death, and eventual recovery. His account is outstanding in its sensitivity and depth of reflection."

—Roger Walsh, M.D., Ph.D., professor, University
of California, and author of *Essential Spirituality:
The 7 Central Practices to Awaken Heart and Mind*

Healing Lazarus
Available in paperback from Atria Books

"[A] stunningly open account."

—*Newsday*

"A gripping and illuminating map of the inner landscape of grave illness, and an ultimately inspiring and tender-hearted return."

—Jack Kornfield, author of *A Path with Heart*

"[A] vivid, affecting, and painfully honest Buddhist dharma (teacher) story. . . . His psychic excavations will enrich all who read this gripping account."

—*Publishers Weekly* (starred review)

"A moving, heart-opening, and gripping account of life taken and regained."

—Daniel Goleman, author of *Emotional Intelligence*

"Compelling. . . . [Richmond's] story's strength lies in the depiction of the arduousness and pain of recovery."

—*Library Journal*

A WHOLE LIFE'S WORK

Living Passionately, Growing Spiritually

LEWIS RICHMOND

ATRIA BOOKS

New York London Toronto Sydney

ATRIA BOOKS

1230 Avenue of the Americas
New York, NY 10020

ISBN: 0-7434-5130-9
0-7434-5131-7 (Pbk)

First Atria Books trade paperback edition February 2005

10 9 8 7 6 5 4 3 2 1

ATRIA BOOKS is a trademark of Simon & Schuster, Inc.

Book design by Ellen R. Sasahara

Manufactured in the United States of America

For information regarding special discounts for bulk purchases, please contact
Simon & Schuster Special Sales at 1-800-456-6798
or business@simonandschuster.com.

To
my teacher and
lifelong inspiration
SHUNRYU SUZUKI ROSHI

CONTENTS

Contents

I SAW MYSELF

I saw myself
a ring of bone
in the clear stream
of all of it

and vowed,
always to be open to it
that all of it
might flow through

and then heard
"ring of bone" where
ring is what a

bell does.

—Lew Welch

Chapter I

WHAT IS WORK?

๛

THE WORD *WORK* has an impressive range of meanings. In ordinary speech, it means making a living, "going to work." In science, it means "the transfer of energy from one physical system to another." Work can sometimes mean something difficult: "This is *work!*" It can also mean to sew, knit, or weave, as in to "work" a knot. It can mean the opposite of play: "All work and no play makes Jack a dull boy!"

It can also mean success: "This works!" Or the way out, as when we "work" our way out of a jam. We "work off extra pounds," get all "worked up," and so on. The variations multiply. The more we study all its variant meanings we find that the word *work*—like *be, come, go,* or *do*—describes something so fundamental that no one definition can fully embrace it.

So when we ask what is the *work* of a human being, which definition should we use? Is our life *working?* Is it, rather than fun, *work?* Are we *working* our life like Gordian knots that we don't know how to untie? Are we *worked up* about our life, or do we just go about it, day by day, hoping for the best?

Or suppose we go deeper and ask, of all the kinds of work we do, what is our most important work? What are we doing here in this world, anyway, where each of us arrives, naked and helpless, with no map or compass, like a trainee in some cosmic Outward Bound program? As we struggle to get our arms around these questions, there are two things we know for certain—today we are here, and someday, sometime, we will be gone. During our time on this planet, what will we do? What is our responsibility—to ourselves, to our family and friends, to our community, our nation, to all people and the innumerable creatures that inhabit the earth, the sea, and the sky? Do we have responsibility for any of it, or is it beyond our power? What do we say? How will we act?

In other words: What is our Whole Life's Work?

∞

The first answer that may come to mind is that our work is to survive. And this is true enough. Survival always has a high priority in life. But is it the only one, or the noblest? And is it the one most uniquely human? We could say that the work of a dog or a cat, a lion or a gazelle, also is to survive. And for us as well—securing food, clothing, and shelter has been the primary work of humankind for much of its history. In that sense we are like our animal cousins. But we are also more: We experience friendship and love. Our need to survive exists in a larger web of relationships, in family, community, and society. If a truck bears down on us as we are crossing the street, the survival circuits in our brains tend to override all else. Just like a dog or a cat, we leap out of the way faster than we can think about it. The same is true when someone attacks our person, our home, or country. At our worst, we behave little better than lions or gazelles. At our best, we are saints. In between is the challenge and struggle to know how to be fully human.

Dr. Seymour Boorstein has pointed out that this difference between the worst and best in human nature is rooted in brain physiology. We now know that the "survival brain"—the brain stem, hippocampus, amygdala, and other low-level structures—is responsible for primitive survival responses, essentially flight or fight. This brain structure is present in all living creatures, even lizards and crocodiles. It is in the "mature brain"—the frontal lobe and cerebral cortex—that judgment, reason, and social emotions such as friendship and love emerge. We may not realize it, but the survival brain, running on instinct and adrenaline, responds two or three times faster than the mature brain. Dr. Boorstein, who spent his early career as a psychiatrist working with prison inmates, and later with couples and families, has seen this in his clinical experience. When we are under threat, we tend to revert to our survival brains. We get angry, we lash out, we fight, or we run and hide. When we don't feel threatened, we love, we care, we grow. Throughout our lives, these two brains coexist, side by side, sometimes collaborating, more often struggling for dominance.

This struggle is hard work and requires some degree of inner development and self-realization. It has always been so. This work has been the subject of all the great wisdom traditions of the world. They were founded millennia ago, when for most people daily life was a constant struggle, without the technology and convenience we take for granted now. So we mustn't imagine that this struggle between old brain and new is a modern thing, a function of our newfound scientific prowess too subtle for the ancients. The tugging match between the survival brain and the mature brain has been going on for thousands of years. It has not been easy. It is still going on. It is work, our Whole Life's Work, the one that applies regardless of time, place, or culture. But how do we accomplish it?

The purpose of this book is to explore the various dimensions of this question, in all its complexity and variety. For that is the unique condition of the human being: We do not know in advance how to do our deeper work. The cosmic Outward Bound program that deposited us here has not given us this information. We might say that the question itself is the answer: Our work is to find out what our work is. But such a circumlocution provides no real satisfaction. This is an issue that generations of philosophers and religious teachers have tried to unravel, with mixed success. Their answers are helpful, up to a point, but they are still their answers, not ours, and for the particulars of our life, the question remains.

It may help to consider work in the plural—*works*. According to the *American Heritage Dictionary,* this means, "the output of an artist or artisan considered or collected as a whole." We go to the library and see the rows of books bound in leather: the complete works of Charles Dickens, of Ernest Hemingway. But imagine some cosmic library in which all of us, in the course of our life, are creating the bound volumes that in the end will represent *our* "complete works," which we shape and develop throughout life. Indeed, shaping is yet another meaning of the word *work,* as when a sculptor "works" clay. Imagine saying "I'm going to *work*" and meaning "I'm going to *work* something pliable, like clay, the way a sculptor does." We are, in that sense, artisans of our own being, authors of our whole life story, shapers of our own existence.

The deeper we go, the more we see that the word *work* has a history of meanings that reaches back to the distant past, to the very origins of our species. In this deeper sense we are all workers of the existential clay in a way that extends far beyond mere livelihood. The primary difference between rich and poor, modern or ancient, is that the affluent seem to have the luxury to confront this life dilemma at a time of their choosing, while those living closer to the ground have little choice but to deal with the life-and-death challenges to their survival on a daily basis.

We say the affluent seem to have a choice, but that is mostly illusion, just as a curtain strung across the center of a room in which two families live provides the illusion that they live separately, and not together. When it comes to the basics, to life versus death, the partition that separates the wealthy from the desperate in today's world is little different from that curtain. All of us, all of humanity, live in one overcrowded room, on one inseparable planet, in an environment of like aspirations and shared fate. Except for outward show, the Whole Life's Work is much the same wherever we go.

∽

While the ostensible purpose of this book is to explore this Whole Life's Work, its collateral mission is to refashion altogether the meaning of the word *work*. These days, when we say "I'm off to work," we mean our paying job; we forget that this use of the word is a rather recent invention, and that for most of human history there was no work separate from all the other tasks of daily life. The various activities that human beings pursue in the course of their lives—to survive, to endure, to raise children, to care for one another, and ultimately to understand our place in this sometimes frightful, occasionally marvelous world in which we are born, and in which we live and die—is the broader concept of work we will use throughout this book.

We pursue this Whole Life's Work throughout our lives, from childhood to old age. It is an enterprise so much wider and deeper than mere livelihood that it probably deserves a different word. But, for lack of a better word, *work* will do, as long as we understand that no matter how humble our station, how difficult our days, this work is by no means trivial: It is the great work of being human. Underneath our struggle to survive, there is a more primal work.

If there is any word powerful enough to supplant *work* in defining this deeper mission it might be *vow*—an idea we will explore in a later chapter. A vow is a commitment that we stick to, that we are willing to see through to the end. A life lived according to a vow is a life consciously lived, in the full awareness of all its difficulties and contradictions. As the philosopher Albert Camus wrote, "Judging whether or not life is worth living amounts to answering the fundamental question of all philosophy." No matter how desperate our straits, no matter how deep our suffering, there is a force deep within us—a vow, perhaps—that compels us to continue. What is it? Whence does it arise? How can we make better sense of our deepest yearning so that our time in this world can be put to its best use?

To answer these questions we need to explore the somewhat unfamiliar terrain of a Whole Life's Work. Why unfamiliar? In a society where three-fourths of the economy is driven by consumer spending, where the omnipresent lure of advertisement encourages us to take a trip, buy a car, try a new perfume, purchase dresses or jeans or shoes or tank tops in the latest style, the implicit message is that there are only two important activities in life—earning money and enjoying leisure—and that the purpose of the former is to finance the latter. Leisure, the messages that blare incessantly from our televisions seem to be saying, is our reason for being. The logical conclusion of this worldview might be that the ultimate goal of life is some sort of perennial Hawaiian vacation.

But as we all know, few people, even the very wealthy, actually adopt such a lifestyle. Intuitively most of us seem to understand that while "all work and no play makes Jack a dull boy," the converse is equally true. A life of all play leads to ennui and eventually depression and despair. Why? There is no easy answer, except to say that our existence seeks a different purpose. We all know the expression "pursuit of happiness," but what does it actually mean? This book advances the point of view that though we may not be able to define it precisely, happiness has something to do with work—not just survival or livelihood, but work in its wider sense, a purposeful activity that advances our individual and collective search for meaning.

So in this redefinition we imagine work not as just another form of leisure, not as a more industrious form of a Hawaiian vacation, not as an artifact of modern prosperity, but as something quite venerable and ancient, which has its roots in the way life was lived hundreds, even thousands of years ago, and in the wisdom traditions of those times. Because I am a Buddhist, well versed in its worldview and teachings, that is the wisdom tradition I know best, but I do not intend this to be just a Buddhist book, nor are the views expressed here solely Buddhist ones. Buddhism, like any other idealistic system of practice and belief created by human beings, is itself flawed. Many of its doctrines—such as lifelong monasticism and second-class status for women—are conditioned by a particular culture or time period. And like every other religion, as it has moved through the centuries from country to country, some of its original humanity and simplicity has been overshadowed by complexities of doctrine and imagery. Besides, I am more interested in exploring Buddhism's future than its past.

The essence of Buddist teaching, in any case, is not in its doctrines but in the living tradition and example of its living teachers. So, rather than quote extensively from Buddhist scripture or commentary, I have chosen to use material drawn from the teachings of contemporary American teachers, especially that of my teacher, Shunryu Suzuki—author of *Zen Mind, Beginner's Mind* and the recently published *Not Always So*. To paraphrase an old Zen saying: The masters of India and China did not live long ago in faraway places—they are here!

I was drawn to Buddhism at a young age precisely because I saw that, of all the world's religions, the teachings of the Buddha more effectively transcended time, place, and culture. From my Buddhist study has come the conviction that our deepest work as human beings is to discover, for ourselves and for others, what it is to be human.

This insight is really nothing more than a return to the core values that were once the stance of humanity the world over, when we lived cheek by jowl with nature, when there was no firm boundary between work and play, when one activity of life—such as raising children—flowed seamlessly into another, and the days were demarcated not by clocks and street lamps but by the sun, the moon, and the stars.

As we bemoan our fifty- and sixty-hour work weeks, as we struggle to further our careers, let us remember that ours is not the be-all and end-all of human societies. In the pursuit of happiness, we may in fact lag behind our ancient brethren, who may have known something important about work and play and all of life from childhood to old age that we, in our unchallenged assumption of an endless staircase to progress and prosperity, may have lost.

In all that is essential, we traverse life in the same condition as we might have thousands of years ago. Regardless of the computers, the cell phones, the supermarkets filled to overflowing with truck-delivered bounty, we have to tread the path of the spirit that knows no ancient or modern, that beckons us to a timeless journey that each of our forebears had to endure, and that we must, too.

THE CONSCIOUSNESS PROJECT

This timeless journey is known by many names. In Buddhism it is known as the Bodhisattva path, or simply the Path. But for this book I have chosen to call it the Consciousness Project. The Consciousness Project is both individual and collective. It is the individual's discovery of how to live his or her life in fullness, in maturity and harmony with others, as well as the collective discovery of all the generations that have come before us and will come after.

Shunryu Suzuki once said, "I am waiting for the island off the coast of Los Angeles to come to San Francisco."

From one of his students he had learned that, geologically, Catalina Island, off the coast of Los Angeles, is moving slowly north, a few centimeters a year, and will eventually reach San Francisco. As a Buddhist priest, Suzuki certainly would have felt a kinship with that kind of time frame. Buddhist literature often speaks of thousands of lifetimes and cycles of millions of years. The Buddhist worldview accepts the vastness of time and space, as well as the gradualness of human change.

Our species has been on this planet for a few hundred thousand years, little more than an instant in the life of our planet and our galaxy. Science tells us these things, but they are inconceivably abstract. What does it really mean for our present life?

For one thing, it means that learning to be fully human takes a long time. It may seem, from the perspective of this century, that many frightful things have happened. But from another view, we are all slowly learning, generation after generation, what it is to be human and how to live together in harmony and mutual respect. From the standpoint of one or even a few generations, this is a slow process, one that can seem to take a step back for every one forward. But sometimes progress is more rapid.

In 1983, a million people marched down Fifth Avenue in New York City in an effort to stop the proliferation of nuclear weapons in the then two great nuclear powers. Today, that particular fear is reduced; something great happened, inconceivable even two decades ago. An awakening occurred: the Cold War ended. The nuclear threat receded somewhat, and we were given a reprieve. That moment showed us what is possible. However, that triumph was short-lived. Today there are new threats, new horrors to haunt us, perhaps even worse than the nuclear threat, which itself has reemerged as an instrument of terror. One step forward, one step back.

We all want pretty much the same things. We want to be cared for, to belong, to be loved, to be healthy and secure. Suzuki would have added that we also want to be awake, to come to spiritual maturity, to be *buddha*—originally the common Sanskrit verb for "to wake up." These are our deepest desires. In the fulfillment of these desires, we—a work crew six billion strong—are pushing on the great island of humanity, moving it inch by inch toward a higher latitude. Of course, some of us may become confused and want to own the island, or blow up the island, or push away those who are of a different nation, race, or religion. This is the darker side of human nature, which slows our efforts.

Indeed, we must not be naive or complacent about the progress of the island. We now have the ability to destroy the island completely or render it uninhabitable by poisoning it or make it too hot or cold. Terrible things are happening in our world; the light and dark sides of human nature are advancing together. The task of pushing the island has become more and more problematic as our capabilities have grown, and there is no guarantee that the island will ever get to its destination.

How can we, in our insignificant, humble lives, contribute more tangibly to this worldwide process of awakening? We are not saints or priests. We work at ordinary jobs and live ordinary lives. What does the grand concept of a Consciousness Project have to do with us?

In fact, each of us has his or her individual Consciousness Project, which is a part of the greater one. This individual project to reach wholeness and spiritual maturity is our life's work, and at the end of our life it will be expressed by all that we have said and done to make our way in the world and leave our mark. These acts of individual authorship have an outward manifestation—we have raised children, pursued careers, made friends, gone fishing, climbed mountains. These are the outward aspects of our whole life.

But for each of these outward acts, there is an inward corollary. In the course of raising our children, we have raised ourselves to a higher level of maturity, compassion, and understanding. In climbing a mountain we confronted our fears and learned something of courage in the face of adversity. In the placid waters of a mountain lake, our fishing pole drifting lazily in the current, we have had a chance to reflect on our life, in the quietude of great nature.

The bulk of this inner work is shared with no one. Consciousness builds and grows over the course of our lives, it

encounters setbacks, in a crisis it may become terrified or confused, but as we come to the end of life all this inner work
becomes the sum total of who we are, the maturity of our years,
the realization or disappointment of our dreams.

In the next chapter we will explore the various modes of outer
work we do in the course of our lives, and the inner work that
corresponds to each of them. This schema—eight modes of
outer work, eight corresponding modes of consciousness—is
the backbone of *A Whole Life's Work* and its organizing principle.

Chapter 2

THE EIGHT MODES OF WORK

❧

WHAT IS IT that we actually *do* in the course of our lives? In what kinds of work do we engage—not just livelihood, but other kinds of work? We do an impressive variety of things as we grow from childhood to adulthood and old age—we raise children, we learn, we teach, we participate in society in various ways. All of this activity takes time and energy; it is arguable whether to call these activities "work" or something else. The point is that, throughout our life, we work at many things, strive in many ways. A comprehensive list of them might be rather long, but in practice we can define eight categories, eight modes of work: Earner, Hobbyist, Creator, Monk, Helper, Parent, Learner, and Elder.

Although at first blush these modes resemble chronological life stages—we begin life as a Learner, progress through various activities of adulthood, such as Earner, Helper, and Parent, and end our days as an Elder—in a larger sense, at every stage of life we have the potential to engage in any one of them. Together they are what define our life and provide it with purpose and meaning.

That is why these modes cannot be mutually exclusive. A Parent may also be an Elder; for a successful novelist, the Earner's Work and the Creator's Work are the same. Each mode of work describes a way of engaging with the world, as does the inner development, or consciousness, associated with each. Furthermore, each mode implies a strategy for making sense of our world and furthering our chances to develop and prosper in it. So, for example, the Parent's Work, which is the most primal of all, anchors our life purpose in something elemental and biological. And by having children, by pouring our love and care into the long task of instructing and raising them, we impart something of ourselves to the next generation, we accomplish a future, we establish a legacy.

ERIKSON'S LIFE CYCLE

In developing this schema of eight modes of work, I am indebted to Dr. Erik Erikson and his theory of the "Eight Ages of Man." The essence of Erikson's theory—which he first outlined in *Childhood and Society* and developed in many later works—is that every stage of life, from birth to death, confronts us with a developmental challenge. If we rise to the occasion and meet the challenge, we grow and move on. If we fail, we stagnate. Probably the most familiar of these eight life stages is the "identity crisis" of late adolescence—a term that Erikson coined—in which the young adult grapples with the questions Who am I? What am I going to do?

The eight modes of work are not quite the same as Erikson's eight stages. For one thing, our modes of work are only loosely

tied to a particular age or stage of life and do not really correspond, in the way Erikson's stages do, to the psychodynamic
development of the human personality. But the purpose of the
two eight-part schemes is similar: to help understand how we
develop and grow and what we need to do to grow well.
Another difference is that while Erikson's orientation is psychological, ours is spiritual. As we see it, the ultimate goal of
human life is not just to be emotionally healthy and contribute
to the well-being of society—though this is certainly important—but to awaken to the ultimate truth that underlies all our
human efforts, to become Buddha. Further, the purpose of this
awakening is not just to be, in a spiritual sense, "the best that we
can be," but to bring others along, to recruit the whole of
humanity in a transgenerational project to complete the gift of
self-awareness—the Consciousness Project.

Now let's examine each of the eight modes of work in detail.

THE EARNER'S WORK. "It's a living," we say with a shrug,
harking back to a time when most people had little choice
about their livelihood. Today the choices are greater, and with
them new problems. David, age twenty-eight, is a software
programmer for a large corporation. He enjoys his work, up to
a point. But the company he works for is, to his mind, unen-
lightened. His bosses are fixated on the bottom line and push
the employees to cut corners in order to meet corporate goals
and deadlines. David yearns for a job he can be proud of, in
which his ethical standards are honored. He is making good
money, but already he finds himself scanning the Internet for
another position.

THE HOBBYIST'S WORK. The word *hobby* tends to belittle
what it claims to celebrate. "Oh, it's just her hobby," we say. In

fact, many people work with more enthusiasm at their hobbies than at their paying jobs. Many hobbies might serve as livelihoods too, but for the hobbyist they are just for fun. Often, hobbies are paths not taken, careers not chosen, former earner's skills still pursued for the pleasure they bring.

Consider Josh, age forty-two, a supervisor at a large hardware store. His hobby is sailing. He owns a twenty-four-foot sailboat and spends many hours every weekend polishing, sanding, and painting—backbreaking labor that would pay poorly in the job market. However, his reward is not money, but the joy he experiences as he sails under the Golden Gate Bridge and out into the open ocean. Although while in college he earned part of his tuition each summer as a member of a yacht crew, Josh knows that now there is no way he can support his family through sailing. But he puts his all into it nonetheless.

THE CREATOR'S WORK. The Creator's Work includes all the pursuits we traditionally associate with the arts—writing, music, sculpture, painting, architecture, and many others. As with the Hobbyist's Work, the Creator's Work might also be a livelihood for some, but artistic careers are difficult and highly competitive. Esther was trained as a concert violinist, but now she makes her living as an administrator for a major symphony orchestra. She still plays her instrument and performs with an amateur string quartet, but because marriage and pregnancy derailed her professional musician's career track, she does not make a living at it. Yet, the joy of making music is still the emotional and spiritual center of her life.

THE MONK'S WORK. The Greek root of the word *monk* means "alone." There was a time in history when the Monk's

Work was an honored vocation in its own right. These days many people hardly recognize that when they take a walk in the woods, or spend a day fishing on a quiet lake, they are practicing a form of the Monk's Work. We all need time to reflect and be alone, and in recent years meditation retreats have become one popular expression of this need, but many people engage in the Monk's Work only involuntarily, when they fall ill or suddenly become unemployed.

The Monk's Work is where we touch our inner selves most directly. Jeanine, finding a pink slip on her desk one morning, decided not to rush back into the job market. Instead, she took the summer off and hiked the Appalachian Trail. She was not especially religious or trained in any formal meditation technique, but that period of isolation cleared her mind and helped her make a decision to change careers.

THE HELPER'S WORK. We are social animals. We live in communities; we rely on and care for one another, and without those bonds we would not survive, materially or spiritually. Some careers—doctor, nurse, therapist, social worker, teacher— are intrinsic expressions of the Helper's Work, but even those not in such professions often volunteer their time at soup kitchens or in hospitals or nursing homes. This is because in our fragmented modern society we need to honor that sense of community and care that lies at the core of human existence.

Charles discovered this only in his fifties. A busy executive, he had never had the time or inclination for volunteer work, but after his wife suffered a stroke, he spent many months on leave from his job caring for her at home. And after her recovery he felt compelled to volunteer at his local hospital, finding that his experience as a caregiver opened his heart to the rewards of the Helper's Work.

THE PARENT'S WORK. People with children devote them-selves to the long and sometimes thankless hours of parent-hood with hardly a thought that this labor is "work." For many, having a family is simply what life is all about. But the true Par-ent's Work is more profound than just washing dishes and changing diapers. In its widest sense, the Parent's Work is the work of all humanity, and now that news reports confirm that only 25 percent of American households have the traditional two parents with children, we know how much diversity there is in the modern exercise of the Parent's Work—gay and lesbian couples, single mothers and fathers, foster and adoptive par-ents, and so on.

Sharon, executive director of a foundation, was a divorcee with no biological children when she became the adoptive par-ent of a learning-disabled Korean orphan. Sharon added this awesome responsibility to her already busy life because she felt a deep yearning to pursue the Parent's Work.

THE LEARNER'S WORK. As any parent or observer of chil-dren knows, a child works hard at learning the skills necessary to become an adult. The Learner's Work is preeminently the work of youth, but it is liberating to discover that even through adulthood and well into old age, the Learner's Work can con-tinue. Medical science has confirmed that those who continue to learn new skills as they grow older remain more healthy and mentally alert.

Mel, age thirty-seven, exemplified this when, after recover-ing from a disabling bout of polio, he decided to enter law school against the advice of those who said he was much too old. He now has a successful law practice, and has proved that the spirit of the Learner can awaken at any time and continue throughout life.

THE ELDER'S WORK. The spiritual virtue of the Elder is wisdom, and there was a time in human history when the Elder's wisdom was vital to the physical survival of any community, as well as the enrichment of its spiritual heritage. Modern society often does not value the wisdom of its elders, but that should not dissuade us from pursuing and expressing the wisdom that comes with the passage of years. We should also remember that wisdom is not the sole purview of the aged; each of us, even children, has wisdom worthy of notice. The phrase "a child shall lead them" reminds us that even the very young sometimes offer their own form of wisdom.

The Elder's Work is often, though not always, connected to retirement. Penelope a retired music teacher, shares her wisdom by leading sing-alongs in convalescent hospitals. It is her daily joy to sit at the piano and watch Alzheimer's patients suddenly lift their heads when the music starts and begin to wave their hands and sing along. Penelope has not let age defeat her; she has discovered a way to express the Elder's Work.

THE EIGHT MODES OF CONSCIOUSNESS

The modes of work we have described thus far are kinds of *activity* that serve to satisfy our needs and express our interests and passions. But beneath all of this is an inner work, a kind of spiritual activity, that complements and supports each of the eight modes of work. These are the eight modes of Consciousness: Precepts, Vitality, Patience, Calm, Giving, Equanimity, Humility, and Wisdom.

Those familiar with Buddhism will recognize that these eight modes of inner work are loosely based on the Buddhist Paramitas, or essential spiritual viritues. There is an enormous body of literature in Buddhism about these Paramitas and the inner practices to cultivate them. It is not the purpose of this book to replicate these teachings—our eight modes do not precisely correspond to their traditional formulations—but rather to redeploy some of their essential elements in the service of understanding the inner dimension of our Whole Life's Work.

THE EARNER'S CONSCIOUSNESS: PRECEPTS

Nearly everyone would agree that a well-developed sense of moral values is a defining characteristic of a mature person, and that the cultivation of sound ethical principles engages us in all our activities. However, ethical Precepts have particular resonance with the Earner's Work, as we will see presently, because of the close connection between livelihood and survival. To survive in the world means to disturb it some way, large or small. To grow grain we must plow the ground. To build a house we must cut the tree. We might call this effect of our need to survive a "footprint." Wherever we walk, wherever we go, we flatten the grass, we leave a mark. Whether our livelihood involves the manufacture of tofu or napalm, whether we have one coworker or a thousand, a footprint of some kind is left behind. Sometimes the footprint is small; sometimes it is huge. Sometimes it is a footprint of disturbance, sometimes one of restoration. Every aspect of human life involves ethical considerations, but they are particularly evident in the realm of livelihood, in the Earner's Work.

Sometimes the footprint is not as crude as David's, whose ethical dilemma was not about pollution or global warming but rather the way in which his company pursued profits at the expense of quality. By confronting this issue even at the expense of his personal security, he was elevating his personal ethics to a higher level, contributing his tiny piece of moral development to the greater purpose of the Consciousness Project.

THE HOBBYIST'S CONSCIOUSNESS: VITALITY

What role did sailing play in Josh's life? We could say that what he did was "just" for fun, thereby treating his passion as something unimportant. Perhaps to an outside observer his passion for sailboats and sailing was on a par with someone else's passion for bowling or pepperoni pizza, but for Josh it was a way to focus his energy on something he really cared about.

Does this have anything to do with the Consciousness Project? Do his Sunday afternoons spent sanding the deck of his sailboat make Josh, or anyone else, a better person?

Perhaps, perhaps not. But without Vitality, without passion, determination, and care, the Consciousness Project would have a hard time advancing. The island would not move, those of us pushing hard to bring it forward would stand in the sun, mop our brows, and say, "Why go on? What's the point?"

Vitality matters.

THE CREATOR'S CONSCIOUSNESS: PATIENCE

By "patience" we mean the quality that leads us to inspiration, or what the ancient Greeks called the Muse. If we imagine that only people who have a special gift can interact with the Muse, we are selling short the assembly-line worker who imagines a better way to stamp sheet metal, or the man with a burr stuck to his sock who sees how the burr clings and invents Velcro.

The faculty of Patience is responsible for much of humanity's material and cultural advances, but in a deeper sense its cultivation brings us closer to those qualities that unite rather than separate us as human beings. The creative power that resides in each of us at root knows no ethnicity, no nation, state, or religion. It is primally human. Patience is what keeps the Sisyphean task of pushing the island of consciousness forward from becoming stale.

THE MONK'S CONSCIOUSNESS: CALM

The Consciousness Project can never advance only by doing. As with the heave-ho of raising a heavy anchor, there needs to be some rhythm to the process. Doing needs to alternate with periods of nondoing, times of calm reflection.

If Jeanine had not taken time off for her hike along the Appalachian Trail, the course of her life, and the decisions she made, might have gone seriously off track. A hyperachiever who never took time off might say, "Jeanine's walk was a waste of valuable time. She should have just plunged into the next thing."

Not so.

THE HELPER'S CONSCIOUSNESS: EQUANIMITY

Often in human history some tyrant, megalomaniac, or religious fanatic has announced, "I am the salvation of the world. Follow me and you will achieve a better life, a more secure existence, paradise in the now or the hereafter. It does not matter how many suffer and die in the effort, the goal justifies all."

Indeed, many have suffered and died to fulfill these madmen's dreams. The Consciousness Project is fragile. It is susceptible to corruption, to misunderstanding and derailment, by those who take it upon themselves to achieve the final goal without the most basic regard for the feelings of others.

Without the vow of helping as the irreducible starting point, the Consciousness Project quickly degenerates into its opposite: unconsciousness and cruelty. In order to really help another, we need to approach the task with a compassion that transcends sympathy and care—a compassion rooted in Equanimity.

THE PARENT'S CONSCIOUSNESS: GIVING

By being a parent, either literally or symbolically, each of us has a ready-made opportunity to cultivate the seeds of generosity and selflessness that are laid down when we are born. There are certainly other ways to express generosity, but being a parent is one of the most direct and courageous.

Sharon overcame her doubts by taking on the responsibility of an adoptive daughter. She felt, she said, that "she had more than enough for herself, and wanted to share it." This sentiment, if it could ever be broadly accepted throughout the world, would do more, perhaps, to advance the cause of the Consciousness Project than anything else.

THE LEARNER'S CONSCIOUSNESS: HUMILITY

In the following statement we hear the voice of self-righteousness: "Listen to me. I am wise. I *know*."

Many times have we heard such utterances from our charismatic leaders, or opinionated friends, or leaders of other countries and cultures drawing on this false self-confidence to justify lying, prejudice, and hate. Contrast this with the humility of the ninth-century Chinese Buddhist monk Chao Chou, who made this statement when he was sixty years old: "If there is a three-year-old who can teach me, I will learn." Reportedly, Chao Chou lived to be one hundred twenty.

Gabe, age seventy-two, recently took up glider flying. He is delighted with the challenges of learning this new, difficult skill at his age. Is it any accident that all his life Gabe has been a person open to other cultures, other opinions and views, and has a broadness of vision and flexibility of spirit that are an inspiration to all who know him?

Humility helps us remember, as we hunker down to push forward the island of consciousness, that though we know much, there is also much to learn.

THE ELDER'S CONSCIOUSNESS: WISDOM

It is tempting for younger people pushing the island of consciousness to turn to the frail, the sick, the elderly, and say, "We do not need you now. You have no strength." And how wrong they would be. Suppose they are trying to push the island in a direction it will not go? All their strength and youthful vigor will be to no avail, unless some wizened older one comes on the scene and whispers, "No, not that way. This way."

We all have the capacity and responsibility to be Elders, not just when we are old, but anytime we have something useful to impart. And we all have an equal responsibility to listen to the Elders among us.

THE CONSCIOUSNESS PROJECT

The Consciousness Project is the great work that underlies it all, an inner substance like tree sap, turning sweet or sour depending on how the leaves and branches are able to catch the light. The Consciousness Project is both an individual matter—the flavor of our single tree—and a collective one, involving the health and growth of the whole forest, the whole of humanity.

When Shunryu Suzuki spoke of the island moving from Los Angeles to San Francisco, he was also speaking of his own vocation and hope. He devoted the later years of his life to that effort, to bringing to America the wisdom that he had learned in his years as a Buddhist priest. He had no special ambition in coming to America, no thought that he would become a great teacher and best-selling author. In his first year here he sat in his small meditation hall all alone. For twelve years, until his death, he pushed on his seemingly small corner of the island, and along the way touched so many people and changed so many lives.

But he did not imagine that his time here was anything special. In fact, he was humble about his abilities. "I have seen many good Zen masters," he once said, "and I don't think I can be a good Zen master, so I should not try so hard."

This is one of the mysteries of the Consciousness Project and our role in it—we never know whether our contribution will be big or small. And ideally, like Suzuki, we shouldn't want or need to know.

We do our part; we do the best we can. That is our Whole Life's Work. And now we begin our journey through the eight modes of work and the eight kinds of consciousness that reflect and support them.

Chapter 3

THE EARNER'S WORK

❧

"WHY DO YOU work for a living?" I asked Frank, a plumber.

"What do you mean?" he answered. "For the money, of course. If I didn't have a job I'd be another one of those homeless guys on the street."

"Why do you go to work every day?" I asked Jessica, a human resources director by day, an artist on weekends.

"It's a living," she said with a shrug.

Livelihood is an activity so basic that it is virtually synonymous with life. Whether we make a living close to life's roots—by tilling the land, fishing the oceans, or hunting the forests, as nearly all our ancestors did—or whether we manipulate stock derivatives on a computer screen in a skyscraper high above a big city, we are all doing the Earner's Work: making a living, receiving a paycheck, securing food, clothing and shelter, and more, if we are lucky. But whether rich or poor, whether we live in a postindustrial society or an agrarian one, our daily energy is consumed by the imperative of every living creature—to survive.

The phrases we commonly use to refer to livelihood—"putting food on the table," "keeping a roof over our heads," "keeping the wolf from the door"—all reflect this imperative that underlies even the most complex and derivative forms of livelihood. As recently as two centuries ago—and even today in many parts of the world—people did not earn a living by receiving money for their labor; they scratched it out any way they could, by tilling their fields, tending their livestock, and engaging in various forms of barter and commerce. Today our connection to these roots is much more abstract: We receive our pay by electronic deposit, and children in big cities sometimes have to be taught that milk comes from cows, not cartons. Still, in our minds, survival is the goal of any livelihood, ancient or modern. We imagine that before love, before friendship, before all forms of social communion, there is survival. To a drowning man or a starving child, there is no more pressing matter than this.

In terms of a single individual, this is how survival seems. However, we are social animals, too, and the self that we seek to perpetuate is also a social self. If earning a living were simply a matter of individual survival, human society would never have evolved into the complex entity we know today. In fact, the relationship between the needs of the individual and the greater needs of the clan, tribe, social group, society, or nation-state is a struggle for survival in a deeper and more cohesive sense, for unlike our cousins in the animal world, human beings cannot survive alone. We have neither the lion's claws nor the fox's keen nose. Alone, we are slow and clumsy creatures. Nearly any beast can outrun us, and some can destroy us. From our earliest beginnings, our only hope has been to join forces, to work together, to make up in numbers and brainpower what we lack in physical prowess.

So, as we explore the nature of the Earner's Work in our postindustrial society, we need to keep in mind its ancestry. When we put in a day's work at a desk in our high-rise office suite, it may seem as though we are far removed from our hunter-gatherer forebears eking out a day-to-day subsistence directly from the land. But the distance between the prehistoric and the modern forms of the Earner's Work is not as great as we might think. Over the centuries, we have worked out a complex system of labor and reward, owner and worker, employer and employee, but in the recesses of our minds, we are still studying the muddy trail for hoofprints, still scanning the sky for signs of rain.

∞

Karl Marx, writing in the early days of the Industrial Revolution, speculated extensively on the working conditions of early humans. He postulated that peoples' "alienation" from their work and the co-optation of the fruits of their labor by those more powerful—chieftains, kings, and feudal lords—occurred very early, and planted the seeds for the conflict between owner and worker that he saw all around him in nineteenth-century Europe. This alienation, he said, has a profound effect on the human spirit: "[When] labor is external to the worker, it does not belong to his essential being; in his work, therefore, he does not affirm himself but denies himself, does not feel content but unhappy, does not develop freely his physical and mental energy but mortifies his body and ruins his mind."

The common understanding of Marx's theory, and one reason for its vast appeal, was the notion that the source of human suffering was in the distribution and exploitation of labor. In fact, Marx was deeply concerned about people's inner lives too, their "essential being" and ultimate happiness, but he felt that this could come about only if there was first a revolution in the way societies were organized.

Two thousand years before Marx, a religious leader named Gautama probed the origins of human suffering. Like Marx, Gautama the Buddha saw the truth of economic hardship and exploitation, but the revolution Gautama envisioned was not in the outer world but in the inner one of the human psyche—in its desires, its self-centeredness, and most of all in its misunderstandings about the nature of the self and the world. He said:

"Birth is suffering, decay is suffering, sickness is suffering, death is suffering. All grasping at life involves suffering.

"What is the cause of suffering? Craving for sensuous experience, craving to perpetuate oneself."

This "craving to perpetuate oneself," Gautama said, was at the root of it all—deeper than politics, deeper than society, deeper than the vagaries of all human and economic relations. And the liberation he taught required long meditation on this craving, to investigate it, understand it, and eventually transcend it.

Marx saw inner liberation as first requiring outer revolution. Gautama's teachings implied that social revolution would naturally evolve from inner transformation. Marx and Buddha would agree on one thing, though: What people want most of all is to be happy. To be well fed, to be free from danger, to be healthy and full of life is our fundamental wish, and the first task of livelihood. But in every generation—including ours— happiness has been elusive. Besides, when we speak of happiness, what do we mean? Material prosperity only, or an inner richness of the spirit?

Though Marx spoke of "alienation" and the Buddha spoke

of "suffering," both were alluding to the same truth: Survival is struggle. The eat-or-be-eaten conflict in all life, and among human beings, is not a flaw of earthly existence; it is its fundamental nature. The Buddha was one of the first to thoroughly describe the moral and spiritual implications of this truth. He taught that we can be liberated from it by becoming fully conscious of and responsible for it. Now, with smokestacks across the world spewing pollutants into the air, we also understand the material implications of this interconnection—that life is one interlocking system that covers the whole earth, the sea and sky, a weave of give and take.

To pursue the Earner's Work in an aware and conscious way, we need to see it in the context of this give and take, a perspective that reveals not just its material side but its moral and spiritual implications as well. Human beings have at last reached the point at which prosperity for all is at least a theoretical possibility, though sadly not yet a reality. At the same time, our increasing efficiency in ensuring our survival is also threatening that very survival. Nuclear power lights our homes, but the nuclear waste is building up, and will be destructive to all life for the next 250,000 years. Do we know what we are doing?

FOOTPRINTS OF LIVELIHOOD

From the earliest days of hunter-gatherers to today's high-rise office suites, our struggle for survival has had an effect on our environment. In order for us to eat the meat of a deer, the deer must die. To till the soil we must first clear it of brush and trees, then break it with plow and hoe. To build a house we must cut a tree. To make a lake we must dam the river. The more we do to ensure our survival, the more we disturb the survival of other beings and things. These, we might say, are our "footprints of disturbance" in the natural world. Before civilization, when people were few and they could clearly see the effect of their actions, they were careful to minimize these disturbances and worked hard to restore them—balancing their "footprints of disturbance" with "footprints of restoration." They prayed to the deer spirit not to be angry. They apologized to the goddess of the earth for breaking the soil. They made sacrifices to the river. And, by intuiting the deeper harmonies of nature, and their long-term dependence on them, they did not take more than they needed.

These were the footprints of ancient livelihood—footprints of disturbance, footprints of restoration. Long ago, our footprints for good or ill were small and could be managed by the people who made them. But the footprints have been growing larger for millennia. In ancient Greece most of the land was deforested, and it has still not recovered. The extinction of mastodon and mammoth might have been due to human hunters. Today we have to contend with runoff and floods from clearcut forests, with carbon dioxide in the atmosphere and harmful chemicals in our rivers and oceans. What's more, it has become increasingly difficult to heal our disturbances, because our connection to them has become much more abstract. When we sit in the kitchen and wrap food with plastic we are far removed from the factory that made the plastic, and we have no idea what was done to the land and sea to bring that roll of plastic to our door. We have no connection to the animal whose meat we just wrapped—it was probably killed in a slaughterhouse—and the effluent from the plastics factory is managed by corporate executives and governments, not by us. Even if we don't use plastic in favor of recycled paper, the plastic sits on the store shelf until some other consumer buys it.

This is now our world.

RIGHT LIVELIHOOD

In spite of this new complexity, we have not completely lost our forebears' sensitivity to the harmonies of nature, and with the resurgence of Buddhism and other wisdom traditions there is a new awareness about the connection between our livelihood, our state of mind, and the wider world. A term from Buddhist teaching is seeping into mainstream vocabulary: *right livelihood*. Right livelihood is part of Buddhism's eightfold path, and originally it meant a profession that did the minimum of harm to other beings. "It has the characteristic of purifying," one ancient text says. "Right livelihood includes fewness of wishes and contentment." Being a butcher, a tanner, or a soldier, for example, was not considered right livelihood, because those occupations are closely connected with killing—the opposite of purifying, which the text goes on to define as "the protection of living beings." Neither would a drug dealer be practicing right livelihood, because making a living from other people's addictions isn't consistent with "fewness of wishes and contentment."

Purifying and contentment—these together make up the footprint of restoration that we make through our livelihoods. Purifying, or restoration, is the outer manifestation of this harmony; contentment is the inner one. The ancient Buddhists understood that right livelihood operates in both these worlds—the psychological as well as the physical. It is not enough, they say, to just practice purifying—minimizing our harm to other beings and, if possible, repairing whatever damage we have done to them. We must also be content with what we have, and not be greedy to accumulate more riches or possessions than we really need. If we must kill deer to live, we avoid killing the fawns, which are the deers' future. If we cut down a tree, we plant two. This is purifying. And if the meat of two or three deer is sufficient to last us through the winter, why kill twenty? If one tree is sufficient to build our house, why chop down ten? This is "fewness of wants."

"Fewness of wants and contentment" means that right livelihood includes our personal relations too. We compete not just with the natural world for our survival but with one another. The psychological side of right livelihood says that when we are destructive and greedy to suit ourselves, that unwholesome state of mind spills over into our personal relations, and eventually to society as a whole.

These principles may be more difficult to define, much less to follow, in today's world. With today's interwoven global economy, how do we know the effect of our occupation on the "protection of living beings"? And in a world where there is a product to satisfy every conceivable human desire, what is "fewness of wants and contentment"? But the principles of right livelihood are still sound, and in the half-century since Rachel Carson's *Silent Spring* first alerted us to the environmental damage we do, the call to right livelihood has been resonating in more and more ears. When civilization was still young, the Buddha understood that to earn your living in a way that does a minimum of harm to the environment and to others, that is conscious of all the effects our presence has on the world, creates an inner prosperity, a fullness of spirit that no pot of gold can match. Now, twenty-five hundred years and billions of people later, this message is as relevant as ever.

IDEALS AND REALITIES

Matt, fresh out of business school in the early 1970s and on the lookout for a socially responsible business, worked for a time at one of the first environmentally conscious paper manufacturers—we'll call it Goodpaper Co.—as a paper trader. Matt was deeply committed to the ideals of right livelihood and felt that by working for Goodpaper he was making a living in an ethically positive, environmentally harmonious way. But he found that the reality was more complex than his ideals. Here's how he describes his work there:

"I learned how much of business was about buying and selling, so it was there I honed my negotiating skills. I was working both sides: On the one hand I was involved in the whole process of manufacturing recycled paper, and on the other I was competing aggressively in the marketplace to get market share by making the lowest bid."

Matt learned what all "green" businesses have to do in order to survive in our world: Ideals have to be balanced by compromise. A green business has to be a viable business as well as green. Matt learned learned a lot at Goodpaper, but eventually he decided that the role he played there was too much on the side of traditional business. He could operate that way anywhere.

So it was with some regret that he left Goodpaper Co. and started his own business, a greeting card company with spiritual themes. It was not easy—starting a new business never is—and Matt soon found that the ethical compromises that disturbed him at Goodpaper were still necessary.

"What kind of compromises did you still have to make?" I asked.

"I tried to run my own business in an ethical way. The themes of the cards were spiritual in nature—everything from Thich Nhat Hanh to Yogi Berra—and we had a wonderful company culture committed to our ideals. But our vendors were another story. I couldn't entirely control them—the printers and paper suppliers—or their business practices. Yet we couldn't print our cards without ink and paper. It was especially difficult when money was tight."

"How so?"

"I was totally dependent on my vendors," Matt replied. "They made the business run. All our noble efforts would have been to no avail if I couldn't pay them. I was honest with them when cash was tight, and explained to them what was happening. Occasionally it came down to: pay the vendors or pay the employees. Sometimes I had to lay people off."

"How did you handle that?"

"People understood the balancing act we had to make. Still, it's never easy when people lose their job. I just did the best to tell the truth to everyone. That was my bottom line."

"You've had this business for over ten years. Overall, how do you feel about it now?"

"I feel wonderful," Matt said immediately. "With all its difficulties, and all the compromises we have had to make, I wouldn't want to do anything else."

This is the inner satisfaction—"fewness of wants and contentment"—that comes from the practice of right livelihood. Even though the practice is not perfect, even though our footprints of restoration do not go all the way to repairing our footprints of disturbance, how much better—for ourselves, for others, and for the world—to have some restoration, however modest, than none at all.

LITTLE THINGS

Matt was lucky; he owned his own business, and regardless of the difficulties of making it a going concern without compromising his ideals too much, he had more control over his livelihood than most people do. Most of us are employees of some larger entity. The most we can control is our immediate work environment and, to some exent, that of the people around us. We have to content ourselves with smaller footprints, with little things.

Wayne, an attorney in a major law firm, was a person of principle, classically educated and deeply concerned about ethical issues. A student of Buddhism, he was fascinated with its ethical teachings. Like Christianity and Judaism, Buddhism has ten major precepts—ethical exhortations not to kill, lie, steal, and so on—but they are descriptive, not prohibitive. In the Bible, God says, "I am the Lord thy God. Thou shalt not bear false witness against thy neighbor." This is an example of a prohibitive precept. The Buddhist version of a similar principle says, "A disciple of the Buddha does not speak ill of others"—a descriptive precept that illustrates how a Buddhist behaves. The Buddhist ethical rules were not pronouncements; the ancient texts that describe these precepts are lengthy discussions between the Buddha and his disciples about specific trangressions. They are more like Socratic dialogues than a set of rules. The Buddha listens patiently to each case of supposed transgression, and based on the circumstances, he explains how a member of the community ought to behave.

"A disciple of the Buddha does not speak ill of others." Wayne took that one especially to heart. Since he was a lawyer, words were central to his livelihood. One day he began to consider the matter of ethnic jokes. He laughed when he heard them and noticed that he even occasionally told them. Then he told me, "I began to consider our use of language, and the difference between language which describes and language which judges. Ethnic jokes are a way of putting one person up and another down, with implicit measurements of worth and value."

So, he went on to say, he decided to stop telling them.

Did anyone else in the law firm notice?

"No," he said.

Then he realized that this was not enough. He had to make it a point not to listen to the offending jokes. And so he did. Whenever he was in a situation in which he sensed an ethnic joke coming, he would explain his new vow and excuse himself. What was the response?

"The response was great. First, people asked, What? Why? How come? And after I explained my considerations, people said, 'Oh, I hadn't thought about that before.'

"Eventually, throughout the office, at least whenever I was around, people got into the habit of stopping themselves when they began to tell an ethnic joke."

We might first conclude that Wayne's effort was a tiny matter in one office in a large city in a larger country. But was it, really?

If we consider the origins of conflict and war in the world— the way in which whole civilizations are brought down, cities and lives destroyed, children orphaned—we have to wonder. Is there a connection between a vow not to tell or listen to ethnic jokes and the ethnic hatreds that fuel nearly all of the world's ongoing conflicts? How do ethnic hatreds arise in the first place? The answer to *that* question might allow us to circle back and reconsider Wayne's effort in a different light.

We could see Wayne's effort as an example of the "footprint of restoration" in the realm of human relations. Though the footprint of his ethical activity may seem tiny in the larger scheme of things, we cannot be dissuaded by that. We never know how many others are making the same effort or in what ways our modest footprints may become magnified—for example, by being published in a book like this one, an outcome that surely never occurred to Wayne when he began his campaign against ethnic jokes.

Little things may not be so little after all. We can't compare a footprint of disturbance with a footprint of restoration by using a measuring tape. Both of them have unseen consequences, but since the footprint of restoration benefits, rather than harms, its consequences can often reach much further, in pleasant and surprising ways. All beings and things want to be restored, to be healed and cared for. None wants to be disturbed or harmed. Disturbance and restoration may be complementary, but they are not equal.

BIG THINGS

Most of us navigate our daily work life with a sense that our ethical challenges are mostly these small things: how we handle money, the way we wield power in an organization, our personal relationships with colleagues, the ethical calculus that weighs the benefit against the harm of various business strategies or decisions.

But sometimes we are faced with starker choices. Consider Richard, a twenty-five-year veteran of a big-city police force. Making life-or-death decisions is part of a policeman's job. Richard chose police work because he wanted to help people, particularly in their crises and times of need, and he considered himself a considerate, compassionate peace officer.

One day, while driving, he heard over the radio that an armed robbery had been committed by a suspect wearing gold glasses and a leather jacket. Suddenly he looked out his car window and spotted the suspect running down the sidewalk across the street, and watched as the man angrily confronted a bystander. Richard called for backup, but then, realizing that the man had a gun and might do more violence, he decided he couldn't wait:

"So I get out of my car, get my badge out and my gun, and say, 'Sir, please step over to the curb.' The guy starts walking fast toward me. I get behind my car, point my gun, and order him again to stop. His hands are in his pockets. I'm thinking, What's going to happen here? I'm waiting to see the gun come out. Maybe he's pointing it at me inside his pocket. But I hold my fire. When he gets to my car he comes around the front and charges me. I swing the door out and shove it at him. That stops him. He runs across the street, where some arriving officers arrest him.

"Later, at the precinct, the arresting officer comes up to me, rolls the six bullets out of the suspect's gun, and shows me where the primer cap on one of the bullets has been hit. The firing pin hit it, but it didn't go off. When did that happen? I sat there thinking, Suppose he was aiming the gun at me inside his pocket, and tried to shoot me? I could be dead. Maybe I should've shot the guy.

"I thought about this a lot, and talked to a senior officer about this, over and over, trying to figure out if I did the right thing. His answer was, Yes, you did the right thing."

Was Richard right to have hesitated in order not to take life unnecessarily, even at the risk of his own?

"To this day I wonder," Richard says.

It was a big thing—his life or the suspect's—and while most of us will not confront such a stark choice in our work lives, the potential is always there.

Richard may have saved a human life. It's hard to imagine a larger footprint of restoration than that. And it was not just the suspect's life he saved. Something happened to Richard, too. He began to look deeper into himself, to do his job differently.

Richard told me that the younger cops look up to him now as a kind of mentor or teacher, an example of how a good cop should be. The suspect in the gold glasses and leather jacket never knew that he owed his life to a cop who was more thoughtful and ethical than most. But Richard's colleagues know—another example of the way our footprints of restoration radiate in all directions, whether we know it or not.

BIGGEST THINGS

Our personal footprints are part of a larger one, the footprint of company, society, nation, planet. But the connection between what we do as individuals and these larger entities is often hard to see. We evolved, like all creatures, to be acutely aware of what is right around us—an attacking tiger, for example. Modern dangers, such as radiation, pollution, and the ravages of overpopulation, are less obvious to our senses and everyday experience. We need analysis, experiment, and education to understand their effects on us.

People often think that the biggest footprints are beyond our control. It's the corporations, the national governments, the despots and dictators who do all these bad things. What can one person do? Vote? Protest? Write letters to Congress? We feel powerless.

If the big footprints were in a world separate from our tiny ones, if corporations and governments were controlled by aliens from another planet, this powerlessness would be real. But they are not. The beings who control the big footprints are just like us, individuals with the same minds, the same tendencies for good or ill, the same lusts and appetites, and the same vulnerability to the corruptions of power.

We have to be honest with ourselves. If we were in their shoes, subject to the same pressures and temptations, are we so sure we would act differently? The sinister multinational corporation that we imagine is the cause of so many environmental ills is only a magnification and distortion of a "corporation of one." And the converse is true as well: The good that people can do emanates and multiplies from the good that one person does.

This is interconnection in its deepest sense: the realization that the whole world, with all its complexity of disturbance and harmony, can fit into a space the size of the human cranium, and while we are not directly responsible for all of it, we are responsible for our corner of it. And what happens in our corner is connected to all the other corners in many ways.

∽∞∾

The Earner's Work is what we all do to survive. In the process—and there is no help for it—we create a ripple in life's pond. Depending on what we do, we create footprints of disturbance or of restoration. The individual's footprint is small, but when combined with everyone else's it is large. We can simply take care of our needs without much thought about the larger footprint, or we can recognize that we are all complicit in the making of it and need to take responsibility for it. Recognizing the inevitability of our individual and collective footprints is the first step in understanding how to walk the world with footprints of restoration, of care, of compassion and love.

We have already introduced the Buddhist word for this compassionate activity: *precepts*. The Buddhist precepts are guidelines for our behavior, descriptions of how disciples of the

Buddha live their lives. While these precepts pervade every aspect of life, they are particularly important for the Earner's Work. In the next chapter we will explore the ways in which the Earner's Work can be a crucible for our ethical development, and thus our contribution to the great mission of our own, and the planet's, consciousness.

Chapter 4

THE EARNER'S
CONSCIOUSNESS:
PRECEPTS

WHAT IS THE RIGHT THING to do? What does it mean to be a good person?

These questions have plagued us ever since the notions of right and wrong first arose in our evolving brains. If we lived all alone on this earth, if we never encountered another human being, if, like the tree sloth or the albatross, we lived out our existence in splendid isolation surrounded by good things to eat, the answer to this question would be much simpler. What is right would simply be what is good for us. What complicates the matter is the presence of even one other human being. The minute there are others, we have a problem. "Hell is other people," said Jean-Paul Sartre. The biblical brothers Cain and Abel would surely have agreed. Their drama, culminating in murder, puts the question starkly: Do we survive at the expense of others, or do we trust others enough to share with them what we have in the hope of a common reward?

What is right or wrong hinges on our ability to answer this question in each situation. Long ago, the general answer to this question became clear: To survive, we must cooperate. And to cooperate, we must contend, again and again, with the question: What is the right thing to do? The more human beings there are on this earth, and the more we understand the web of interconnection that joins every form of life on the planet, the more the complications of this ethical dilemma abound.

Thoughts of right and wrong, good or bad, begin early in life, in the way we relate to our mothers. We think: When her actions please us, that is good; when not, that is bad. This attitude may seem self-centered, but even as infants our understanding of good and bad is defined by our relationship with another person. Recent experiments have shown that at six weeks infants smile when they see a human face. Precepts grow from there. As we grow older, we see how much our well-being is connected to the welfare of others, and we come to realize that a self-centered view is self-defeating. Gradually we extend this insight to our families, friends, and colleagues—an increasingly wider circle. And so we grow through many stages of moral development, until we reach the pinnacle recognized by all great philosophers and religious teachers: What is good for everyone—for the whole world and its complexity of beings, people, and things—is right, regardless of whether it is good for me. And what is bad for this universe is wrong. I am but a tiny dust mote in it, doing my tiny part to benefit everyone. My action may benefit me in this larger sense, but that is not why I do it. "Me" has ceased to be the issue. This is the stage of transcendent ethics, the highest stage. It is not easy to attain.

DO NO HARM

It is the oath of all physicians and healers and also an ethical principle common to all the world's great religions—*first, do no harm*. Ethical people, we are told, do not kill. They do not lie, cheat, steal, or engage in sexual misconduct. They avoid offending others, don't covet what is not theirs, respect their parents and God. Religions have expanded these principles into vast commentaries on how these principles should be applied to every detail of daily life. Much of our Old Testament is about the minutiae of ethical behavior.

But beneath all this complexity there is this single underlying principle: *Do not harm*. Or, if we must harm, harm as little as possible. Religions have waged holy wars throughout history about all manner of things, but on this issue there is remarkable unanimity. Nonharm, which the ancient Hindus called *ahimsa*, is the ethical ground. And when we must harm, when disturbance is the only option, when we must kill the deer or starve, then we must work to restore. This principle is deeply embedded in our primeval consciousness. It is the stuff of life itself. Life wants to live; that is its defining wish. We are alive; that is our wish too. Do no harm, not because a Sunday-school teacher told us so but because if we clearly experience that we are all one, why would we want to harm anything?

Yet, there is no survival without disturbance. Just by being here, we are disturbers of the peace, meddlers in the wider harmony of being. We kill other animals to eat. We destroy habitats. We plow over and under. Our footprints of disturbance stride on, leaving their marks everywhere. When other feet want to set down where ours are, we have conflict, even war. To ensure our survival is to diminish the chances for something else to survive. There is no free lunch on planet earth for any creature.

The living system that supports us operates according to a principle of conservation of biological, social, and spiritual energy. Each of us perches on one end of a seesaw. For one person's end to go up, somewhere the other end must go down.

The Jains, a religious sect of ancient India contemporary with the Buddha, took this idea of a footprint of disturbance literally. They carried brooms with them wherever they went, sweeping aside insects on the path to avoid stepping on them. They also strained their water through a cloth before drinking it, to avoid ingesting the tiny creatures that lived in it. Similarly, Buddhist monks of that era did not farm, because of the harm they might do to the worms and other creatures of the soil. Instead they begged for their living, primarily from farmers who cut into the ground and grew grain on the monks' behalf.

We must respect the purity of these efforts, but no matter how hard we try—and in the service of an ethical life we must try—we cannot entirely get rid of our footprint of disturbance. Even if we try to make our footprints as small as possible, the result may only be to make someone else's footprint larger. Harm is so interwoven into the fabric of life that, in the end, to call it disturbance is too one-sided. Disturbance, we might say, is the song of life.

What does it sound like, this song? Is it garish and discordant? Sweet and pure? What is the proper attitude when we listen to it? Should we lean to one extreme, and like the Jains emulate a life of asceticism? Or should we stride forward confidently, ignoring the tiny beings underfoot, and try to control the world? In attempting to preserve the spirit of right livelihood, do we self-consciously limit ourselves to jobs and careers that seem to cause a minimum of harm, or do we accept whatever jobs come our way and try to transform their disturbance as best we can?

Richard, the policeman whom we met in the preceding chapter, once came to the Buddhist center where I was the leader. After the morning meditation and lecture, he confided his occupation to me and asked me what he thought Buddhism might have to say about police work.

It was the first time I had ever been asked the question. "I think police work could be a very good job for a Buddhist," I said. "You're really on the front lines, helping people in their most difficult moments." Then I paused. "I think if it were I, though, I'd have a hard time carrying a gun."

Years later, I ran into Richard again, and he told me how helpful my earlier response had been in allowing him to continue his work. "You gave me a real answer," Richard said. "Especially the part about carrying a gun."

A few years ago, some whistleblowers in tobacco companies leaked confidential documents to Congress confirming that their employers knew about the effects of nicotine as early as the 1960s. These revelations led to class-action lawsuits and may well save many lives in the future. If these employees had said to themselves, "I can't work in a tobacco company. It causes too much harm. I'm leaving," who would have been left to blow the whistle?

People have different responses to the song of life, with all its complexity of right and wrong, good and bad. For some, the dissonances in the song of life are too harsh. "I'll tiptoe through life as carefully as possible, causing as little disturbance as I can," these people say. This emulates the Jains, sweeping insects out of their path as they walked. Or maybe in life's song we hear bold Wagnerian harmonies that tell us, "Generating prosperity for ourselves and others is the best way to make people happy." This is like tobacco company executives, who felt they were pursuing the American ideal of capitalism and profit, employing thousands and enriching their stockholders, as they marketed products that their researchers told them caused cancer.

But the song isn't selective. If we want to hear the song as it was actually written, we have to hear all of it. Shunryu Suzuki stressed this point over and over whenever he discussed the Buddhist precepts. His approach was that the precepts were important, but could not be followed rigidly. The song of life, he seemed to be saying, never repeats itself. Each situation arises fresh. In his words:

"If you try to observe the precepts, this it not true observation of precepts. When you observe the precepts without trying to observe the precepts, this is true observation of the precepts. Our inmost nature can help us. When we understand the precepts as an expression of our inmost nature, that is the Way-as-it-is. . . . On the other hand, we want to observe our precepts. We feel that the necessity of observing the precepts will help us, and when we understand the precepts in this negative or prohibitory sense that is also the blossoming of our true nature. So we have a choice of how to observe precepts, one negative and one positive."

Suzuki acknowledged our ordinary understanding of the precepts as rules—do not kill, do not steal, and so forth. But for him, ordinary precepts were just the starting point; he asked us to go even deeper, to transcend a black-and-white attitude toward the world, and rely on our "inmost nature," the heart of deepest compassion that understands the dictum "First, do no harm" not as a rule but as a universal principle and necessity of life, like food, like breathing.

Relying on our inmost nature allows us to practice the precepts more intuitively, as each situation arises, without having to consult a rulebook. Real life is rarely black and white. Shades of ethical gray confront us constantly. Rarely is a situation either wholly good or bad; rarely can our actions be classified as wholly right or wrong. When we strive to dig up "good," "bad" comes up also. Ethical gold is rarely pure.

Suzuki went on to say, "Precepts are not rules set up by someone. Since our life is the expression of our true nature, if something is wrong with that expression, then Buddha [another name for our "inmost nature"] will say that this is not the way."

⁓∞⁓

The Buddhist precepts in Suzuki's understanding are not rigid commandments. The Jains tried to make them so; their effort was extraordinary, even heroic. But what if the Jains lived today, in the light of modern science? They would realize that for all their effort, in each ounce of soil there were even tinier creatures, too small to be seen, or that in the water they so carefully filtered there were organisms that could slip through the most tightly woven cloth? When does such an effort become too much? When do we lose our way in our haste to find it?

Suzuki's comments try to address these questions. However, some may still ask: What is the right thing to do? In the early days of his time in America, someone asked Suzuki just that question. What happened next has been told and retold for years as part of the lore of the San Francisco Zen Center and of Suzuki's teaching. Although I was there that day, I can't say that my account is what *really* happened. Perhaps no one can say for sure. But here is how I remember it:

After Suzuki's Saturday-morning lecture, the question-and-answer turned to the Vietnam War. There was a big antiwar demonstration that day, and many of us who were actively opposed to the war were conflicted about being at the Zen Center instead of the demonstration.

Someone began the questioning by asking, "What is war?"

Suzuki immediately pointed to the three-by-six-foot bamboo mat on which two people were sitting in front of him, and said, "When you sit down, each person tries to smooth out the wrinkles under where they are going to sit. When the wrinkles meet in the center, that is war."

Suddenly the room burst out with excited questions: "How can we stop the war?" "Shouldn't we go to the demonstration as engaged Buddhists?" "How can merely meditating stop suffering in the world?"

As the questions went on and on, Suzuki appeared to have difficulty following the students' rapid-fire English.

Finally, thinking to clarify what was going on, a senior student raised his hand and said, "I think what we are asking is, What is the right thing to do?"

Suddenly Suzuki leaped up, his robes flying. He jumped off the lecture platform and began beating the student on the shoulder with his teaching stick. "What are you dreaming?" he shouted.

Then just as suddenly he sat down again, his face ashen, and said, more quietly, "I'm not angry."

The silence that filled the room was electrifying.

This was one of the few times he had ever done something like this. Usually he was so gentle, so kind. I was shocked. I had read about Zen masters of old beating their students on occasion, but I had no idea it was still done. I thought, Either this man is off his rocker or his understanding of the world is leagues beyond mine. Should I follow him or my activist instincts?

After the lecture, I saw Suzuki off in a corner talking quietly with the senior student he had beaten. Much later I learned from others who knew him well that for a moment he was indeed angry, in spite of what he'd said. In private he had explained that the raft of questions about the Vietnam War had brought up in his mind all the pain, frustration, and helplessness he'd felt as a priest in Japan during World War II. His reaction was, at least in part, a very human one.

Today, I look back and think that he was saying, "You are asking, 'What is the right thing to do?' You're asking *me,* as though I have some kind of rule of thumb, ready to hand to you on a platter? What are you dreaming?"

That was the day I decided to follow him.

⌘

Some of the frustration we all felt that day was the perennial one: How can I, as one person, with no power to influence great events, do anything? The suffering that pervades the world seems bigger than any one person or group of people can change and rolls on like a careening juggernaut. What can I do?

The answer has to come partly from the rational mind, and partly from deeper mind.

With the rational mind we can see that the interconnection between events and things is deep and thorough. The effluent from fertilizer factories in St. Louis flows into the Mississippi River, out into the Gulf, is carried by ocean currents to the far corners of the world, and affects the fertility of penguins in the Antarctic. We may even understand that the abuses of power we see in our offices are small examples of the large abuses of power that occur throughout the world between ethnic groups, nations, between the world's rich and its poor, between the haves and the have-nots.

But to see how our tiny individual actions can have an impact on this web of connection we need to go beyond rational thinking. Long ago, the Buddhists developed a visual metaphor for this extension of awareness. Imagine, they said, a vast net, like a fisherman's net, in whose every knot is a bright shining diamond. And imagine further that if we were to peer into any one of those diamonds we would see reflected an image of the whole net, with all its myriad diamonds stretching everywhere in time and space.

This so-called Net of Indra teaches us how to see ourselves as able to make an impact, because each of us is one of those diamonds. In our bright crystal essence we reflect the light of all the other diamonds, as they reflect ours. What we do in our work and how we deal with the ethical considerations that confront us every day are reflected on the whole net, and influence its overall brightness.

From within the confines of our individual cubicle of work and life, we are permanently logged on to this ethical internet, and the messages our actions send are picked up and received by all the other nodes. There is a connection between disrespecting a colleague at work and polluting a trout stream, a link between corporate bosses who abuse their power to enrich themselves at their employees' expense and the way powerful nations impose their wills on weaker ones.

We saw this in the story of Wayne, the attorney we met in the last chapter. Harm begins in the mind. An inappropriately large footprint of harm has its genesis in unknowing, in ignorance and lack of awareness. The trivial and the not-so-trivial ethical dilemmas of the modern workplace—the compromises on quality to increase profit, the exploitation of employees in the service of shareholder value, the abuses of office politics and power—are experiences, at the personal level, of the universal fact of harm. Even when the effort to minimize harm is taken to extraordinary lengths—as with the Jains—the problem of harm does not go away. Life in the Jains' time was simple. In the Earner's Work of the modern world, it is much more difficult to see how large our footprints are in the world. So we can neither ignore the harm we do nor, if we are at all ethically developed, be complacent about it.

These days, of course, we cannot sweep the sidewalk with a broom, and our drinking water is purified long before it comes out of the tap. A purist approach is what impels some people to seek out occupations that appear to cause a minimum of harm—working for a religious organization, for example, or an organic-food cooperative. The example cited above of the whistle-blowing tobacco executives shows another way to exercise precepts in the workplace. Once again, as the senior student asked Suzuki, we must ask: What is the right thing to do? On what basis do we make those decisions?

STAGES OF MORAL DEVELOPMENT

We all know that children are not born with a fully developed moral sense. In fact, the young child has very little concept of morality except as it pertains to his or her needs. The child thinks, What is good for me is right; what is bad for me is wrong. Child development experts have extensively studied how a moral sense develops as we grow to adulthood. Some think that moral development is learned behavior, like language, while others believe that it grows as an adjunct to the emotional bond we have with our parents. Whatever the mechanism, it is clear that morality develops gradually as we mature, and that not all adults reach the same level of moral understanding.

We understand, as adults, that morality is partly expressed by laws, customs, and religious principles such as "A disciple of the Buddha does not harm" or "Thou shalt not kill." But it is only at the highest level of ethical maturity that we come to thoroughly internalize these principles. When we reach this level, morality is no longer a matter of self-interest, or of gaining others' approval, or even of conforming to the norms of society. The ethical standard becomes something transcendent and universal. It is only in rare individuals that these moral principles become paramount and trump all concerns for self-interest. Gandhi is one modern example. In his philosophy of *satyagraha,* or nonviolence, any thought of self-interest or protection is overruled by selfless devotion to a higher truth.

It would be gratifying to imagine that in every situation we can act from the highest stage and follow the ethical standards of all great religions and all spiritual teachers. But we know that this is not so, especially in the realm of livelihood. The circumstances under which we earn our livings are too important—and on occasion the ethical lapses we encounter too egregious—for us to easily set aside our needs for survival, for fairness and dignity, in the service of an ethical standard that is far higher and loftier than that of those around us. In practice, the highest stages of moral development—"Do unto others as you would have them do unto you" and "Turn the other cheek"—are ideals, beacons to help guide and orient us as we struggle to contend with the ethical challenges that face us.

CARRYING THE BURDEN LIGHTLY

This state of affairs could be cause for pessimism. While most of us strive to live moral lives, we see examples of amoral and unethical behavior all around us—in our personal lives, in the workplace, in society and world at large. But in the face of our own and the world's ethical imperfections, we must not become discouraged or lose hope. To know these facts and to become weighed down by them, sometimes even to the point of depression or despair, is actually just another way of avoiding our proper responsibility. To say, "Oh, this is too much. I don't want to take on the burden of the world's dark footprint," is an understandable reaction. But the world's dark footprint need not be only a burden.

This world is the only world we human beings have. We must find a way to love it regardless, the way we would our only child. Amid the darkness, we must remember how to laugh. Amid sorrow, we must remember that there is also joy. Amid great suffering, we must understand that while things may not be the way we wish them to be, at least things are the way they are. Isn't that how we would regard our only child, with unconditional acceptance? The way things are provides us, always—and this fact redeems so much—with a starting place.

In Buddhism we have Avalokiteshvara, whose name literally means "the one who sees," or, more poetically, "hearer of the cries of the world." Avalokiteshvara is a saintly being who hears the suffering of everyone in the world—the celestial Bodhisattva of compassion. Can we imagine such an all-encompassing awareness and empathy? We can barely stand our own suffering, much less that of six billion other souls. Why does Avalokiteshvara not succumb to despair? The visage Avalokiteshvara is always portrayed as serene and peaceful. Avalokiteshvara exemplifies the Buddhist teaching that the highest form of compassion is equanimity, an even-mindedness that includes the embracing of all sorrow, but that is not brought down by it—an attitude to which we can all aspire.

One time, after a Buddhist lecture I had given, a woman

raised her hand and explained that she worked as a home nurse for a person with Lou Gehrig's disease. "He's not going to get better," she said. "And he is in such despair. What can I do?"

Having just recovered from a long illness myself, I thought back to a time when I lay helpless in a hospital bed, and tried to remember which of the nurses' actions was most helpful to me. Finally I replied to the woman, "Of the two of you, you are the one who has a choice about despair. Just be yourself."

I remembered that of all the nurses who cared for me, the ones who were the greatest comfort to me didn't try to do anything special; they were just themselves. In the end, that is the best we can do, especially in the workplace: be ourselves, as fully as we can in each situation, recognizing that each day of the Earner's Work, each encounter, has in it some flavor, however faint, of Avalokiteshvara, hearer of the world's cries.

The footprints of disturbance, even of harm, are everywhere, covering so much of the world's ground that, in the spirit of Avalokiteshvara, we might try to see them also as footprints of restoration. Why should we do so? How can we fathom such a contradictory notion? Because in the end, if there is any good at all in the world, where else but amid our suffering and mistakes are we to find it?

PRECEPTS AND THE
CONSCIOUSNESS PROJECT

Each of the eight modes of consciousness is a branch of the tree of the Consciousness Project. The role of precepts is to help us know how to make our contribution to the Consciousness Project in a way that causes as little harm as possible to the world and to ourselves. There are many ways to push on the island of consciousness. Some of them push the island backward, into chaos and darkness. We must work against this. We must try to find the best way to go. After all, the island of which we speak is not a physical island but one that is created in our minds. Each of us is responsible for his own direction. Unless we push with care and compassion for all that is around us, the island will founder.

QUESTIONS TO ASK, THINGS TO DO

What Is Happening?

His Holiness the Sixteenth Karmapa, a Tibetan Buddhist and one of the great spiritual teachers of our time, looked up from his deathbed and said to those who were near, "Nothing happens."

To comprehend the deep meaning of this cryptic statement, we might need to spend a lifetime (or several lifetimes, according to the Tibetan way of thinking) in spiritual study. Lama Surya Das, an American who studied with the Karmapa, interpreted his comment this way: "Everything changes, and yet at another level, in the realm of absolute Being, nothing happens. It's a double-edged statement. We live in birth and death, moment to moment, but every moment, nothing happens. You could say it's the ultimate long view, and the basis for patience and forbearance."

But in a mundane sense, the Karmapa's comment is simply an invitation to actually *see* what is happening. The first step for any effective action, particularly in regard to the footprints of harm we know are all around us, is simply to *see,* to notice clearly what is going on. So often we are tempted to rush into action before we have taken this critical step.

In your place of work, for example, what is actually going on? What do you see? Beneath the surface and petty distractions of daily activity, what is really happening? What is the company's mission? What is the true intention of a colleague who appears angry or frustrated? How is your work connected to the larger fabric of company, society, and planet?

We must remember that the literal meaning of the name Avalokiteshvara, the Bodhisattva of Great Compassion, is "the one who *sees*." How can we have compassion for anyone or anything, much less act in the service of positive change, if we are so confused or caught up in our personal views and prejudices that we cannot see what is actually going on?

"Nothing happens": We might understand this as an utterance by someone who sees the world and all its woes so clearly and transparently that it appears to him as one great ocean whose surface waves are subsumed in the infinitude of its stillness. This is the eye and the heart of Avalokiteshvara, the activity of compassion at its highest level.

Suppose we ask, "That's fine for the Karmapa. But what about an ordinary person like me? How is some saint's cryptic deathbed utterance going to help me get through the day?"

None of us is ordinary.

What Can I Change?

"The world and its confusions are too vast and intractable. What can one person do?"

This is the plaint of would-be and burned-out activists everywhere. But to this question there are two obvious answers:

First, we can always change ourselves. Change one diamond on the net and the change is reflected everywhere.

Second, one person can always do something. Finding something to do is not really the problem; the problem is that we imagine our actions are somehow irrelevant or insignificant and therefore we do not engage in them.

Remember Wayne the attorney's refusal to tell or listen to ethnic jokes. Irrelevant or insignificant? Look what happened: First he changed himself, then he changed his colleagues. Then he told me, and now I'm telling you.

Nothing is insignificant.

Pick One Thing to Do

"This company is a jungle. Management is unreachable. Everyone is ducking for cover, or out for their own enrichment. Our products harm the environment. I've got to get out of here, find a better job, anything but this hellhole."

Perhaps. But what is in front of you? On your desk? In your latest e-mails? Who is in the next cubicle? What could you say?

Pick up a diamond, any diamond.

How Far Are You Willing to Go?

Not everyone is ready to be a hero, at least not all the time. The first rule of livelihood, as we have already discussed, is self-preservation.

This was Richard the policeman's moral dilemma, confronting an armed criminal with a gun in his hand. His first responsibility was to himself, his survival. But as someone with a well-developed moral sense, he also knew that if he gunned down the criminal prematurely, or without compelling reason, he could not live with himself.

The criminal approached. Richard's finger closed on the trigger.

How far was he willing to go?

Richard found his answer in the press of life-or-death circumstance. Each of us has to do the same, in his own time, his own way.

Chapter 5

THE HOBBYIST'S WORK

❧

THE WORD *HOBBY* is rather inadequate for the range of activities it describes. It seems connected with childhood, and memories of collecting stamps, dolls, and baseball cards. Even when it is applied to the adult world, with its wider variety of pursuits, the word remains slightly undignified. Would that there were a better word, but even the thesaurus has little to offer besides *pastime, pursuit, leisure activity,* and *avocation.*

So it seems we are stuck with *hobby.* What are hobbies? Why pursue them? In what way do they deserve to be dignified by being included with the other, apparently more meaningful modes of work?

Wayne, in addition to his work as an attorney, has several hobbies. When we hear that among them he counts bird-watching and stamp collecting, we may think, Well, if he finds it relaxing . . . without wondering what these pursuits mean to him. Wayne himself says:

"Very often sound is the first clue to presence of a bird. Then some motion. Where? Above that tree, which one? Is it a tree, a shrub? What color is it? How does it sit on a branch, 35 degrees or upright? What is its bill shape? Plumage pattern? Eye color? Habitat? Where is it perching? Ground? Midway up? Exposed branch? Deep inside?

"I didn't start watching birds until I was forty, and after I had become hooked on it, I thought, The birds have been here all along, where have I been? It was a way of observing things closely, and of looking at my life as a whole."

This description goes far beyond the notion of a hobby as something we do to relax in our spare time. Wayne speaks eloquently of his passion for birds, the fine details of the craft, and most of all the way in which it has had an enhancing and transforming effect on him. I asked Wayne whether he felt that the word *hobby* was inadequate for the full scope of the activities he described, and he said no. His attitude was not to let the narrow focus of the word detract from the significance of his birdwatching, but the reverse: to let the magnitude of birdwatching's effect on him dignify the word.

After this description, I could well understand Wayne's fascination with birds. But when he told me that one of his other hobbies was stamp collecting I wasn't so sure. What was the significance of stamp collecting for him? "When I was a boy, my father gave me a big globe, which I still have today. He got letters from all over the world, and in addition to collecting the stamps off the envelopes, I would go to the globe to find the places. Sometimes my father would help me. Philately, the official word for stamp collecting, means 'love of distances.' Through stamps, and map reading, I learned to visualize the larger world."

Wayne may be more articulate than most in describing the inner significance of his hobbies, and his descriptions help us understand why hobbies can be so much more than "leisure pastimes." Wayne's hobbies engage all his energy and passion. They help him integrate and pull together disparate aspects of his inner and outer lives. They evoke pleasant memories of childhood and family. And most important of all, they stretch and expand his definition of self.

Not every hobby has this effect, certainly. For some people, a hobby may indeed be little more than a leisure pastime. Others may say that they don't have a hobby or have little interest in acquiring one. But even for those people, if we ask, "Besides your paying job, what activity in your life do you pursue with passion, that you find exciting and engaging and worthy of many enjoyable hours of your time?" most would have an immediate response. Perhaps that should be our working definition of a hobby in its wider sense: a passionate pursuit, one that makes life come vividly alive.

NOT A PAYING JOB

We all know that a hobby is an activity for which we are not paid. The minute someone pays us for it, it's a job. That's one of the qualities of a hobby we most enjoy. Not only are we not paid for it, but no one tells us how to do it. Since it is our living, one might think that we work hardest at our livelihoods and devote less energy to our hobbies. But sometimes the reverse is true. The freedom to pursue a hobby for its own sake, without any complications of money or authority, sometimes means that we apply ourselves to our hobbies even more diligently.

One of Richard's hobbies was playing the violin—Richard,

the policeman who confronted the armed robber in an earlier chapter. His only compensation was the pleasure he took in doing it: "I wanted to play the violin all my life but I always thought I didn't have the talent to do it. Reading music and playing all the notes seemed so difficult. And then recently I met this violin teacher, a young man who told me not to worry about all that. He was more of a bluegrass fiddle player, but very good. He got me started playing tunes on the violin more or less by feel, and now it's just about the most enjoyable thing I do."

Paul, now a much-in-demand recording engineer, was for many years the owner of an auto repair shop. During that period he pursued sound engineering in his spare time. It was his hobby and more: He devoted every available hour of his nights and weekends enhancing his equipment and perfecting his skills. Eventually musicians heard of Paul's work. One found out about him by listening to his recording of a local symphony. The man was so impressed with the quality of the work that he called the radio station to find out who had engineered the recording. Soon, so many clients were coming Paul's way that he was able to sell his auto repair business and become a full-time sound engineer. Now Paul has all the pressures of a paying job—negotiating fees, meeting deadlines, satisfying paying customers. The work started for him as a hobby. Now it's his livelihood.

When I asked Richard why he was trying to teach himself the violin at the age of fifty, he replied, simply, "I love the violin." When I asked Wayne that question regarding his bird-watching, he said, "When I am on the trail with my binoculars, all my senses are engaged. I am fully alive." As for Paul, when I asked him about his engineering, he said simply, "Music is my life."

Clearly, a hobby is indeed a "passionate pursuit." It engages all of our energy. How does this compare with a paying job? Do we find that same passion, that energy and zeal, that we find in our hobbies? Sometimes we do. Arnie, a physician, said to me, "I love being a doctor so much that sometimes I think I'd do it even if I weren't paid for it." Richard is passionate about some parts of his job, too: "I became a policeman because I wanted to be of service, to help people, and that part of the work—as opposed to the bureaucracy and the politics—I'm still passionate about. When we go to an apartment where someone has just died, the people there look to us as their only hope in a desperate situation. Being there for people in that kind of circumstance is why I became a cop."

But realistically, many of us aren't able to find or sustain that kind of passionate involvement in our paid employment. It's just a job, after all. For most of us, going to work is, well, *work.* And a hobby is, by contrast, play. Work and play: This seems to be the critical distinction. When work is *work,* it's not a hobby. When work is play, it's something else altogether.

PLAY

The most common response when we ask people why they engage in their hobbies is, "It's fun!" Hobbies are activities that we enjoy. Even if we find our paying jobs fulfilling and rewarding—as Arnie the physician did—we cultivate our hobbies not just because they are fun but because they are *only* for fun. With a hobby, there are no complications—no bosses, no evaluations, no unions, no bureaucratic paperwork, no company rules, no politics, none of what makes many paying jobs so frustrating. In the pursuit of our hobbies we are our own bosses. For many, the Hobbyist's Work is as close as they will ever come to the satisfaction of being self-employed. Because our hobbies aren't our livelihood, we don't have to worry about pay cuts or layoffs. We get to enjoy all the satisfactions of a paying job without any of the frustrations.

Play, like *work,* is an elemental word with many shades of meaning. But we know what it is at its root: doing something for fun, not caring about the outcome, an activity with no stakes attached, such as tossing a Frisbee on a lawn, playing Monopoly or Scrabble, or clowning around with the dog. Play is a state of mind, an attitude of not taking things too seriously. In play we have a sense that the bindings that organize the world are loosened. To be playful is to be carefree, happy, bubbling over with the enjoyment of being alive. When we are sad we cannot be playful. In grief, play vanishes. People who are depressed lose their ability to play. And since so much of childhood is concerned with play, for an adult to be playful is to be like a child again, to encounter each thing in the world as though it is fresh and new.

Work and play appear to be opposites. But when we think of the labor involved in pursuing a hobby, it is not quite so. In chapter 1, we mentioned Josh, the hardware-store supervisor who owned a sailboat. Why would Josh spend his weekends sanding the deck of his sailboat—hot, physically exhausting work that he could have hired someone to do for minimum wage? Similarly, why would Wayne traipse through muddy forest trails, in the early morning cold and damp, binoculars hanging from his neck, for a glimpse of a rare bird? Because when it is what we love, and it is free from constraints and conditions, work ceases to be *work,* and becomes play.

We should not be surprised. The conjunction of work and play is evident in children from a very early age. There may be no time in life when we exert ourselves more than when we are learning to walk. We stumble, fall down, bounce back up, take a few more steps, stumble, and fall again. But we do not give up. Even before we can speak we have an intense, ingrained desire to learn this skill so necessary for survival. And that intensity persists throughout childhood. Anyone who spends time with children cannot help but be struck by the passion and total commitment they invest in their games. In considering children's games, what may appear to a casual observer as chaotic activity—"a lot of yelling and screaming," in the words of a woman who rose at a community meeting to register her objections to a planned playground—is actually a sign of children's continual work at learning the skills they need to grow up.

Part of why we pursue our adult hobbies with such passion and vitality, then, is because they are fun, because they are a kind of play. In that sense, hobbies are a subset of the larger category of leisure and entertainment.

LEISURE AND ENTERTAINMENT

The natural play of children and adults that has existed in every culture from time immemorial has, in our society, now been thoroughly commercialized. Sports, television, movies, popular music, restaurants, nightclubs, Club Med, Walt Disney World—we live in an entertainment universe! When we ask people what their hobbies are, they sometimes refer to a form of entertainment—football, for example. And such people can be as passionate about football as Wayne was about birdwatching. Indeed, games and entertainment have always been a part of human societies, and often have been connected to religious observances and festivals.

Today, of course, entertainment is largely divorced from community celebration and has become, like a Rolex watch, just another article of consumption. We are supposed to think that the reason why we work is that it enables us to afford to play. We imagine the wealthy as those who can live their whole lives in leisure—lying outdoors in a hammock, dozing the afternoon away. In leisure we imagine we can do whatever we want—even do nothing at all.

Why are hobbies and their cousin, leisure, so important to us? The naive answer is that work is stressful, even unpleasant, and that leisure is the antidote. Why else do people eagerly anticipate their three weeks of paid vacation (six weeks in Europe)? The notion of leisure time has become so embedded in our daily lives that even to pose these questions seems strange. Everyone loves free time. It's what we work for, isn't it?

And yet if we ask people, in the middle of their entertainments and leisure activities, why they are doing them, they often answer, "Otherwise I'd be bored!"

BOREDOM

"Why are you playing that video game? You've been playing all day!" the parent asks her child. The child answers, "I'm bored!"

We think of entertainment as an antidote to boredom, without stopping to consider what boredom actually is. Is it a specific mental state or an absence of one? When we are not doing anything in particular—when we are neither happy nor sad, nor irritated or pleased, focused or distracted, alert or tired—we may say we are bored. If someone asked us to describe our mental state at that moment, we might shrug and demur. "I don't know," we might say. "I just feel at loose ends. I don't have anything to do." The statement implies that having something to do is generally more desirable than not being occupied. Boredom signals a desire to be in a condition other than the one we are in, to be stimulated, to be active—indeed, to be entertained. When we are bored, we pick up a book, or turn on the television, or go to a restaurant or movie or nightclub or bar.

In the same way as leisure stands opposed to work, boredom stands opposed to doing. But we need not languish in that realm—not in today's world. Today, the entertainment industry stands ready to assuage our every millisecond of boredom. Its offerings are stunning in their variety, for children and adults of every age. These entertainments have become so central to our lives that it requires an effort of will to step back and ask the not-so-obvious question: What is really so unpleasant about boredom?

One answer is emerging from recent neurological research. It seems that in addition to familiar drives such as food and sex, there is one called "seeking," which is essentially the desire for something new, the desire to do new things. We seem to have deep in our brains a circuit that is wired for novelty—perhaps because creatures that explore their environment, "sniff out" new aspects of it, have a better overall chance to survive.

But the story of human evolution is about how we have transcended our primitive drives. Now that meditation, "just sitting," has insinuated itself into the culture, and so many people are pursuing meditation in the hope of enriching or transforming their lives, the question of boredom takes on new significance. By any ordinary definition, meditation ought to be the most boring activity imaginable. Sitting still doing nothing, watching the breath, attending to bodily sensations—the polar opposite of Disney World! And yet, for those who do meditation, it isn't boring. The outward circumstances that might once have triggered the thought, Oh, this is boring! now have become interesting.

We ought to wonder why. For when we set aside outward

activity and distraction, when we quiet our attention, the inner whisperings and workings of the mind gradually emerge, like shy creatures coming out at night. And then we begin to understand: What we thought was boredom, and what made us want to turn on the TV, pick up a book, find anything to occupy our time, was in fact only the no-man's land between the outer and the inner life, that twilight zone where the sunlight of activity has faded but the moonlight of inner life has not yet risen. If we are patient enough to wait out this so-called boredom, we find that eventually another world, one populated by the entertainments of our own mind, opens to us.

It may seem trivializing to say that one of meditation's roles in our hyperactive world is to redefine boredom, but it is not. It is an important factor in meditation's new popularity. The intensity and variety of activities—some of them dangerous—that people will do to avoid that twilight zone of boredom is staggering. The engine of the consumer society and its distractions is driven in large part by this surprisingly powerful desire to avoid, at almost any cost, the twilight zone and what might lie beyond. How might a society look whose citizens have learned to reach beyond boredom to the more authentic interests of intimacy, care, and the perambulations of their own minds? It may not be reaching too far to say that a society such as ours has a vested interest in keeping boredom at bay, for fear that our artificial wants might shrivel, and our authentic desires might flower.

RESPITE AND LAUGHTER

Having said all that, there is still a vital role for entertainment and leisure in our lives, if only to give ourselves respite from the demands of the human condition. Before there were Barbie

Dolls and Game Boys, there were shadow puppets and rag dolls. Before there were movies, there were jugglers, story-tellers, circuses, and mimes. There has always been a rightful place for entertainment, not only as diversion from the human condition but as drama and high art to illuminate and disclose it. Without respite the human condition would overwhelm; without comedy and laughter there would be too much seri-ousness and grim resolve. Dr. Arthur Deikman, in his studies of religious cults, notes that one of the characteristics of a cult is lack of humor, especially of the self-deprecating kind. Religious life that is too strict and rule bound can easily turn sour and devolve into oppression. Our society is exploring one extreme of affluence, entertainment, and frivolous pursuit. Other soci-eties, in other times and places, went the other way. Our Puri-tan ancestors are only one example, and even today there are religious groups and leaders who rail against the "permissive-ness" and "moral laxity" of our Cineplex society.

In our best moments, we realize that neither extreme is healthy. We need a bit of both, we need to satisfy both the hedo-nist and the ascetic within us. The highest entertainment and the highest wisdom join at the point of honest laughter, which is our unique birthright. We share many qualities with our ani-mal brethen, but laughter, it seems, is uniquely ours.

LOOSENING THE BOUNDS OF SELF

Our hobbies and entertainments can evoke an energy and vital-ity that is deeper than mere pleasure. As Wayne said, "The birds opened a door for me, helping me to get past my narrow preoc-cupation with self and begin to look at my life as a whole." This "opening door" means loosening the bounds of self, connecting us more deeply to the world and to others. It is a gate, perhaps, to that more profound transcendence of self that Buddhism teaches, though the authors of ancient Buddhist texts might look upon bird-watching or stamp collecting as frivolous distractions. But the concept of passionate pursuit was certainly not foreign to Gautama the Buddha; in fact, his life path provides a shining example of zeal.

Perhaps our more modern passionate pursuits can, if considered in the right way, be a kind of "dharma gate" into that same spiritual world. And why not? The great twentieth-century Buddhist scholar Edward Conze remarked, speaking of the Buddhist wisdom tradition in *Buddhist Thought in India,* ". . . About five centuries ago . . . spiritual creativeness began to wane, and no authoritative religious work of outstanding genius has been produced since that time." Dr. Conze's comment demonstrates the respect he had for the ancient Buddhist tradition. But it also encourages us to find ways to restore that creativeness and make that tradition more relevant to our modern world.

The central tenet of the Buddha's spiritual teaching is that clinging to a narrow sense of self is the source of our suffering, and that knowing a wider, transcendent being is the gateway to liberation. Meditation—or, more precisely, just sitting—is one method for cultivating this experience. Through sitting in stillness we expand the bounds of our narrow self and come to see ourselves and the world more generously—from the standpoint of what Shunryu Suzuki called "big mind."

Thirty years ago this meditation experience was largely missing in the West. But it is not uniquely Buddhist. In fact, sitting in stillness may be the most universal spiritual experience of all, transcending culture, time, and place. In *The Real Work,* Gary Snyder wrote of the basic quality of meditation: "Primitive people and animals . . . are capable of simply just being for long hours of time. [It is] a completely natural act. To the contrary, it's odd that we don't do it more, that we don't, simply like a cat, be there for a while, experiencing ourselves and whatever we are, without any extra thing added to that."

This experience is not—or was not—something rare or unusual reserved for monastic professionals, but a common potential of all humanity. It simply requires the willingness to do it, time, and energy—especially energy.

When Wayne said, "The birds opened a door for me," he wasn't *meditating* as such, but bird-watching was a way for him to loosen the bounds of self—a kind of meditation. But it was not the relaxed do-nothingness of Homer Simpson in his hammock; it was intense. Just to *be* there, all the way, takes energy. We can't have the full experience of watching the bird, as Wayne described, by watching one on television. We have to *be* there. That is the deeper meaning of passionate pursuit, and the reason why our so-called hobbies transport us out of ourselves, even if only a little. Although our avocations might seem superficial or trivial to others—Wayne said he had to overcome the stereotype of bird-watching as something for "sissies and little old ladies in tennis shoes"—the passion we bring to them may bubble up from a deeper, subterranean stream. The river running in the underground of the spirit may provide the energy for our work, our hobbies, and our deepest spiritual aspirations.

The experience of being fully human is larger than any one tradition or teaching can ever encompass, and if it is true that each of us has the innate nature of a Buddha—an awakened one—then the seeds of that awakening should be abundant, accessible, and easily discovered, like acorns covering the ground in autumn, for those who have eyes to see them. The key is to have the passion, energy, and perseverance to look, as Wayne did when he followed the rustling in the tree branches until first he saw only a glimpse of plumage, then finally the whole bird.

In our avocations and pastimes, the seeds of awakening are there. And what after all best exemplifies the quality of awakened spirit? A pinched, crabbed attitude toward life, one steeped in self-righteousness and denial, or one suffused with the spirit of play, of simple enjoyment of the bounties of life and of one another?

As Ryokan, the seventeenth-century Japanese poet and Zen monk, wrote:

> Day after day
> The children play peacefully with this old monk.
> Always two or three balls kept in my sleeves,
> I have had too much to drink—spring tranquility!

Chapter 6

THE HOBBYIST'S CONSCIOUSNESS: VITALITY

A PASTIME LAZILY PURSUED is soon forgotten; an avocation tried out of mere curiosity quickly grows tiresome. Vitality is the quintessence of an authentic hobby. The avid Hobbyist is above all passionate about his craft. I once attended a business conference with a man who—once the business conversation was out of the way—began to talk about his true passion: tuna fishing. I listened to him for more than fifteen minutes while he went on and on about the hypnotic deep blue of the Caribbean waters, the intricacies of bait selection, the thrill when the hooked fish first broke water, and the physical tug-of-war between man and fish. Then, probably because he noticed the expression on my face, he stopped and said, "You're not a fisherman, are you?"

"No," I replied. "But you certainly seem passionate about it."
He rolled his eyes in mock ecstasy and said, "You have no idea."

In contrast, I think of my father, a keen believer in various forms of self-improvement. I can remember him at various times taking up bridge, the clarinet, mambo dancing, tennis, hiking, stock market analysis, and chess. But each time his enthusiasm was short-lived. The energy for these endeavors was lacking—the clarinet and the books on bridge and dancing soon disappeared, and after his death at age seventy-six, it was left to me to discover these relics of his brief enthusiasms gathering dust in my mother's garage.

Clearly, something more than a surge of initial interest is needed to sustain a real hobby, something that comes not from the mind and the realm of ideas but from the heart. In discovering a true hobby, the initial spark of interest quickly expands into a deeper fire, which draws on fuel that often is abundant enough to last a lifetime. A true hobby leads to a total engagement during which the individual nearly forgets the self and its preoccupations and enters a realm of joyful surrender to his or her chosen task.

We might call this kind of energy or passion "worldly vitality," in contrast with its more rarefied cousin, spiritual vitality. Buddhist teaching recognizes that spiritual vitality is one of the essential ingredients on the path to awakening. If the spiritual aspirant isn't at least as excited and passionate about spiritual liberation as the sailboat enthusiast is about making headway in a stiff breeze, the Buddhist practitioner would have about as much chance of success as my father with his clarinet.

Though it is true that any activity passionately pursued superficially resembles the spiritual vitality of which Buddhism speaks, surely this worldly vitality must be several orders of magnitude removed from the profound surrender of self taught by the Buddha as the gate to liberation. How can the elation felt while sailing have anything more than the most superficial resemblance to the intense desire for spiritual liberation felt by the Buddhist practitioner in deep meditation?

Indeed, the connection may seem quite a stretch, except that Buddhism itself, as it developed and refined its doctrines and practices leading to liberation, makes the same sort of connection. It is with this sensibility that we can say that the passion with which my business acquaintance pursued tuna fishing is of a piece with the passion with which the Buddhist meditator pursues enlightenment; that the singleminded concentration with which Wayne observed birds through his binoculars is not fundamentally different from the zeal with which the spiritual aspirant observes her inner states of mind. Of course, tuna fishing is not spiritual liberation, nor is bird-watching meditation. They are what they are. But if the capacities needed for the enlightenment that the Buddha taught were not already present in the mind of every human being, if the seeds were not there, then his message of universal liberation would have no meaning. Zeal for tuna fishing is not fundamentally separate from zeal for enlightenment; the mind of bird-watching is of a piece with the mind of meditation. We have, in the end, only one mind. There is, in the end, only one reality.

Shunryu Suzuki loved the metaphor of the garden. "The most important part of spiritual practice is the preparation of the ground," he said. "If the ground is good, the seeds will naturally grow." Chogyam Trungpa, like Suzuki a pioneer in bringing Buddhism to America, was even more earthy. He likened our ordinary experience—our suffering, confusion, and pain—to excrement, the nourishing manure that allows the tree of wisdom to grow. In the experiences we think of as least spiritual—in our anger, desires and passions, greed, lust, and sorrow—we will discover the raw material from which the mind of the Buddha can grow.

The Buddha is nearly always portrayed in paintings and sculpture seated on a lotus, a beautiful, pure flower that grows in murky water. The symbolism is clear: Ignorance and liberation exist in one integrated ecosystem, each nourishing the other. The seeds of spiritual awakening are everywhere. Our hobbies, trivial though they might seem to others, are near cousins to the deeper passion that fuels the most fundamental work of our life, or, as Suzuki said, our deepest desire: to be awakened, to be Buddha.

EXPERIENCES OF VITALITY

You sit down before a blank sheet of paper, or close your eyes and visualize the inner blank slate of your memory and recollection, and try to remember ten moments in life when you felt the most alive, the most vital. What would you write? What would you remember?

Perhaps it was a sports moment, the memory of catching a football and running all the way downfield for a touchdown. Perhaps it was the first time you urged a horse you were riding to a full gallop, and felt the wind in your face, your hair streaming behind you, the power of the running animal under you.

Or maybe it was a moment of danger. An old soldier might recall the moment he and his platoon charged over the top of a hill directly into enemy fire, yelling like demons, adrenaline pumping, their fear transformed into heroic action. Someone else might remember walking down a city street one night and being confronted by a man with a gun, her whole body pulsing with incredible energy while her mind became unbelievably focused, her speech paradoxically calm and clear.

Maybe someone else would recall gyrating and shouting at his first rock concert, or being swept away by his first time falling in love. What about the joy of running down a deserted beach into a rosy sunset, or diving into the icy waters of San Francisco Bay?

There are as many answers to the question as there are people. What seems to be the common thread in all these experiences, however, is that they have some relationship to our fears and desires—fears when we are able to muster the courage to overcome them, and desires when we are able to fulfill them.

Physiologically, this is not hard to understand. In both cases our heart pounds faster, our mind focuses, all extraneous distractions fall away, and we enter the state of being fully alive. In these moments we are totally one with what we are doing. There is no time or space for reflection, for equivocation or doubt.

Spiritually, however, some distinctions need to be made. Not all experiences of vitality are equal, just as not all fears and desires are commensurate. The desire to be rich and famous, for example, while common enough and certainly in the mainstream of human experience, is quite different from the desire to be one with God. The fear of being socially embarrassed is not quite the same as the fear of dying.

VITALITY AND DESIRE

There are many varieties of desire, some trivial, some profound, but a few—like the desires to survive, to procreate, to have enough to eat—are universal, part of our genetic script. Others—such as the desire to help others, or the desire to acquire spiritual wisdom—are more rarefied, and typically cannot fully blossom unless our other, more primeval desires are dealt with first. At least, this was the thought behind psychologist Abraham Maslow's formative theory of the "hierarchy of human needs." He posited that a hungry peasant scouring the hillside near his home for enough firewood to survive the night is unlikely to be much interested in political science or religious philosophy, at least until he has had his meal.

In its effort to understand and legislate various aspects of human desire, Buddhism at least implicitly acknowledges this theory. The explicit moral rules it teaches—do not kill, lie, or steal—make clear that unless we corral our cruder impulses and desires, however energizing and vitalizing they might be, we will never be able to live together in harmony or experience liberation.

Suzuki's statement, "Our greatest desire as human beings is to become Buddha," is interesting for two reasons. First of all, it tells us that the desire to become Buddha—that is, to be fully conscious, fully awakened—is in the end a desire like any other and shares certain qualities with all desires. Second, it makes clear where the desire to become fully conscious stands in the hierarchy of desire—at the top. As Suzuki explains it, not all desires are equal, but all desires are desire. There are various kinds of desire, some base, some noble, but what unites them all is vitality. If a desire—any desire—does not carry with it an intensity, an energy, a zeal for its satisfaction, then it hardly deserves the name. Furthermore, any desire intensely felt must have some connection with the king of all desires: the desire to be fully conscious, awakened, to accomplish our piece of the Consciousness Project, to be Buddha.

But it is not easy to develop the desire and passion to be Buddha. Until recently in the West, Buddhism was something to be learned only from books. And even now that there are, present among us, masters of the various Buddhist traditions well schooled in their practices and willing to teach others, relatively few individuals actually make the effort to find such teachers, or pursue the long, arduous path of study that they recommend.

But what of the vast majority of humanity, who have no interest in the Buddhist way, who follow their own religions with passion and diligence, who look not to themselves for spiritual satisfaction but to God? What of those who have scant interest in anything spiritual and only wish, in the words of one of Joseph Heller's characters in his novel *Catch-22,* "to make the time go slow," that is, to live as long as possible?

Is the Consciousness Project only for the spiritual elite, those who understand the nature of the island of consciousness and of the task to move it northward, or is it for everyone? What chance does the Consciousness Project have for ultimate success if many of those who inhabit the island have no interest in the island's ultimate destination, especially since its forward pace of a few centimeters a year is hardly perceptible and certainly unlikely to benefit us within our lifetime?

VITALITY AND THE SEARCH FOR MEANING

At the beginning of this book we said that we do not come into this world knowing what our work is. The cosmic Outward Bound program that deposited us here has not supplied us with this information. We know this work has something to do with the Consciousness Project, but the specifics of it are still unfolding. If we are correct that this great work of life is something universal, transcending culture, society, educational level, and affluence, then we should see its signs everywhere, in every person.

It is sometimes said that the goal of Buddhist practice is to answer the question, Who am I? What you will eventually discover in meditation, says the Buddha, is that you are not a separate being, an "I" floating alone and isolated in the great sea of Being, but are that very sea of Being itself. That is who you really are, says the Buddha, and that realization has the power to liberate you from the deep, existential suffering and anguish in the depths of the mind that you were born with. Shunryu Suzuki, with his penchant for simple explanations, called this sea of Being "big mind." But he also took care to add that the need to realize big mind was not a criticism of "small mind." Small mind and big mind, he taught, are two facets of the same jewel.

VITALITY AND THE
CONSCIOUSNESS PROJECT

The Consciousness Project is the goal of all humanity. And if it fails—which it might—it is not likely to be through lack of imagination, since imagination is our strong point. No, it is more likely to fail through loss of zeal, sheer exhaustion at the difficult effort to be fully human. In the end, it is not the smartest or the quickest who wins this sort of race. Smartness is what has brought us to this pass, where the whole world may crumble from our inventions, weapons, and pollutions. Those who will win this race are the ones who will stay with it, who have the vitality and the grit to persevere, who will not look back or give up.

Buddhism calls these warriors of the spirit Bodhisattvas, literally "enlightenment beings," and what fuels their passion is their vow never to cease their efforts until all beings are fully awakened. They are construction workers of the inner life whose hobby, we might say, is enlightenment. They love what they do, and they are not celestial beings, as some Buddhist scriptures would have it, not exalted beings from elsewhere in the firmament.

They are each of us.

QUESTIONS TO ASK, THINGS TO DO

What Is Your Passion?

Not all of us have well-defined hobbies as Wayne did. Sometimes the subjects of our true passion are hidden in other activities or are somewhat undeveloped. Ask yourself: What is my passion in life? What makes my heart sing?

If it is your job, if you are pouring all your life's energy into your career, then that is the answer. But then you might ask yourself a follow-up question: Is this a good thing? Is it healthy and fulfilling to have all of your life's energy devoted to your livelihood, or is there some kernel of a "passionate pursuit" outside your job that could be cultivated, bit by bit, as you go? If all of your energy is focused on your job, what will you do if you lose it? Or when you retire? Many work-focused individuals feel at a loss when retirement comes; they have not developed a parallel track that can serve them throughout their lives.

How Is Your Passionate Pursuit Connected to the Search for Meaning?

Some people are passionate about gambling; others, sports cars. These are all right, as far as they go. We all need our diversions. But for our avocations to have some connection to our Whole Life's Work, they need to have some intimation, however distant, of that larger work.

Take stock of your pursuits, and consider in what way that connection is there, or can be strengthened. Think of Shunryu Suzuki's metaphor, "The most important part of spiritual practice is the preparation of the ground." The deeper purpose of our passions is not so much their subject—they could be anything, from butterfly collecting to cooking—but the passion itself. That passion can help prepare the ground, so that when the time comes to shift the focus of your passion to your life itself, you will be ready.

Chapter 7

THE CREATOR'S WORK

❧

THE TERM *Creator's Work* makes us think of music, painting, theater, architecture, dance—the creative arts. The arts are certainly one form of the Creator's Work, but the work itself is broader and deeper. Creativity is a faculty as innate as language—our ability to imagine, and then make real, that which does not yet exist. We are innovators by nature.

Originally this talent helped us survive. Whoever fashioned the first bow and arrow was, as we say today, thinking outside the box. For most of our history, innovation has kept us going. But even when our lives don't depend on it, the Creator's Work remains important, if not for physical survival, then for mental and spiritual wholeness. The Creator's Work is a fundamental attitude we bring to life—a spirit of openness, receptivity, and freedom. The Creator's Work questions the status quo, tries things out, and opens us to new possibilities. It keeps us flexible and gives us confidence that whatever our setbacks and disappointments, we can continue to shape our futures—"every breath, new chances," as an old Zen saying goes.

We need to distinguish between *applied* creativity—poetry, painting, and sculpture—and *innate* creativity, which is the creative impulse before it has taken specific form or shape. Innate creativity is clearly evident in young children. Naomi, an artist, had this to say: "I love working with very young children as they draw and paint. Until they are four, they are completely pure in their creations. They draw a line, using their whole arm, and say, 'This is Daddy.' And then another line, and say, 'This is Mommy.' Their vision flows onto the page without any preconceptions. After that, adult expectations and standards creep in, and the children start to lose that freedom."

Naomi is right: We may never be more purely creative than when we are young. Young children don't differentiate between the inner world of imagination and the outer world of the senses. They haven't yet been trained to do so. In modern society, what adults generally touch on only in dreams, children experience while they are awake. In the ancient world, there was less distance between the mind of a child and the mind of an adult. Arthur Koestler has theorized that as recently as the period of classical Greek civilization, the division of psyche into conscious and unconscious was still incomplete, so that when Socrates spoke of the "daemon," his voice of inspiration, he actually heard it, speaking inside his chest. Dream and waking life, impulse and rational thought, have separated only recently, Koestler believed.

The rational waking mind that we now consider normal is fashioned by years of formal education. Even creativity itself has been tamed by conservatories and art schools. But creativity in its purest form still seems to operate independently of education, following the contours of brain evolution and consciousness. When I asked John, a professional composer, about his creative process, he said, "I go to the place where music is, I listen, find what I want, and bring it down into the world." John had a formal education in music, but I doubt that what he described was something he learned in the conservatory. If a five-year-old were as articulate as an adult, he might say the same thing about his imaginary creatures and games. The experience of creativity is an encounter with the Other, a place larger than self, where we connect with the sacred and the divine.

The American Museum of Natural History in New York displays reproductions of cave paintings more than twenty thousand years old. The drawings show horses, bison, antelope, and people, all drawn with extraordinary grace and mastery. We do not know what purpose the ancient artists had in depicting these scenes—whether the works were connected with some hunting ritual or religious observance—but the images demonstrate the power of the essential creative act.

As Gary Snyder says, "The cave tradition of painting, which runs from thirty-five thousand to ten thousand years ago, is the world's longest single art tradition. It completely overwhelms anything else. In that perspective, civilization is like a tiny thing that occurs very late."

∽◌∾

The ancient painters picked up a piece of charcoal or ocher and recorded what they saw and felt—not unlike Naomi's four-year-old who drew a line and said, "This is Mommy." Her teacher might have said, "That doesn't look like your Mommy. Can you draw a face on her?" But the four-year-old's drawing is not a representative image; it is a gesture connected with the creativity of life itself, whose power and potential are always available to us.

TALENT

In most people's minds, the idea of creativity is connected with *talent*. Parents and teachers use many words to describe a child destined for success: *smart, gifted, high aptitude,* but most of all, *talented.* Talent is real enough, as every professional in the arts knows. But the idea of talent can also be limiting, even oppressive. The poet Robert Creeley tells of a poet friend of his who was once asked, after a reading, "Is that a real poem, or did you just make it up yourself?" The questioner apparently thought, as many do, that "real" poets are different from those who just write poetry, "real" inventors from those who just tinker, "real" writers from those who just scribble. What is this difference? Who defines it and decides it? By the standards of classical piano, jazz great Thelonius Monk did not have much facility. Who was the more talented painter, Picasso or Grandma Moses? Talent, like so many other things, exists partly in the eye of the beholder. Were the Paleolithic cave painters *talented?* Were they "real" painters, or did they just paint? As Naomi says, "Every country in the world has fantastic folk art. The Balinese have an extraordinary artistic heritage—rituals, crafts, and dance—but until the tourists came they hardly thought of it as art. It was just their life."

Sometimes talent emerges where we do not expect it. Jeff had a frustrating childhood. His teachers said he was a slow learner; he was dyslexic, teased in school because he seemed "dumb." But from an early age Jeff had magic hands. His parents and others who were close to him understood this, in spite of his difficulty in school. He would fashion wire coat hangers into jet planes, glue scraps of wood into elaborate castles, and, later, build exquisite model ships from scratch, using hand tools.

When he was sixteen Jeff was caught stealing car stereos. His arrest was a critical turning point; there was a danger that his talent might turn sour and be used in the service of lifelong self-destructive behavior. Fortunately, he received timely counseling and professional help for his dyslexia and attendant emotional problems.

Today Jeff works at a film studio, helping construct robots and models of spaceships. His magic hands have become his livelihood. Just as very few people can paint like Picasso, very few have a way with machine tools like Jeff. He does not talk much about his craft, almost as though talking detracts from the work. When I asked him about it, he said only, "I like making things." Nor does he speak of his difficult early years; he says only, "I finally figured out what I could do well."

Jeff clearly had talent, once it was finally recognized. But what was his talent? And more to the point, *where* was it? In his hands? In his brain? In his perseverance and luck? And what about the rest of us? Are we all arranged on a cosmic bell curve of talent, with the unendowed at one end and the geniuses at the other? Or are we all talented, but in unique and different ways?

Perhaps it is both. Some people can write a "real" poem, one that skillfully expresses a feeling or an idea and honors the aesthetic standards of the art. But others "just make it up," because all of us can speak, and everyone has something to say. Naomi says, "There is a term for art that people just do—*outsider art*. This is the work of prisoners, mental patients, and other people who have figured out what they like and want to do. They can have tons of creativity, especially when their beliefs inform their art. For Native Americans, their art was all about their beliefs, and that's the best art there is."

In the realm of *applied* creativity, talent rules, and some have more than others. But *innate* creativity is a different matter. Innate creativity is universal.

EVERYDAY CREATIVITY AND INVENTION

In our daily lives, we can see many examples of innate creativity that have little to do with traditional ideas of talent. When we decorate our homes, detail our cars, lay out our gardens, make up bedtime stories for the children, we are using our innate creativity—making our own personal works of art. These works don't hang in museums, but they are made from the same raw clay as those that do. Life is full of these modest efforts.

Everyday creativity starts with the self. From time immemorial, the first palette of self-expression has been the body. Tattoos, cosmetics, jewelry, and body piercing all say, "Look at me! I am different!" The fads and fashions so important to teenagers, the hard work they put into their ever-changing hairstyles and clothing, remind us that the struggle for identity and self-expression begins with the body. Adults extend this process by personalizing extensions of themselves, including their homes. We hang our own paintings and photographs on the walls; we decorate the rooms with shapes and colors that suit our tastes; even the scraps of paper stuck to the refrigerator door tell a visitor that this is not just any house, but ours.

The automobile—that American icon of individualism and freedom—is another area where creativity blooms. We have low riders, high riders, chrome exhaust pipes, detailing, and now the latest fashion—neon! Those who think of their cars as utilitarian objects hardly worthy of notice must remember that in some city neighborhoods, the customized car is as much an expression of individual creativity as is a poem.

It is when everyday creativity extends beyond the private and into the public sphere—when it is placed in the service of the whole community—that creativity becomes invention. All the artifacts of modern life, from the kitchen match to the nuclear reactor, were invented by someone. The whole story of civilization, from the mists of prehistory to the present day, is a chronicle of creativity and invention. There was a time when the cultivation of grain, the wheel, the bow and arrow, the beast-drawn plow, the bread oven, and the forge represented major advances in the quality of human life. Invention is the territory where the inspirational and the practical converge.

Necessity is the mother of invention, so the saying goes. Invention has been to our advantage in the battle for survival. Without tools, human beings are weak and vulnerable creatures. Naked against a predator, we don't stand a chance. But when we see a stone on the ground next to a hard nut, we know how to pick up the former to crack open the latter. We know how to sharpen a stick to make a spear. It is the inventors among us who have transformed our planet into a self-constructed habitat—beginning with the plow, the wheel, the bow and arrow, the forge, and continuing today with the supercomputer, genetically engineered corn, the space station, even the nuclear bomb.

But not all invention is driven by necessity. Left to our own devices, we don't sit passively against a tree waiting for hunger or a predator to come. We are curious creatures. If we see a knife next to a piece of wood, we whittle. If we're swaying rhythmically back and forth as we pull up a net full of fish, we sing. If we see a cave wall illuminated by our flickering torches, we draw.

Why do we whittle rather than leave the wood alone? Why do we sing when silence would do? Why do we paint bison instead of just watching them roam? Why do we tell stories about wolves that can speak and fish that can fly? We do so because our innate creativity is always active, constantly pulsing, continuously at work.

CREATING CONSCIOUSNESS

Invention is the Creator's Work put to the common good in the world we share. But our creativity does not rest there, nor does its purpose end with our death. This is where we part company with other creatures. We are conscious beings, and our innate creativity is at work in that sphere too.

The highest use of the Creator's Work is not in the clothes we wear, the cars we drive, or the inventions we make, but in the shaping of our psyches. This inner sculpture begins when we are born and continues until we die; it includes the material, the psychological, and the spiritual. Our parents and society provide the raw material; the happenstance of our lives continues the process. At some point we grow up, we are on our own, and from then on the kind of person we become is up to us.

Our innate creativity is probably much what it was in the days of Cro-Magnon man. In fact, Cro-Magnons' brains were somewhat larger than ours. The rise of civilization from their time to the present has not been because our brainpower has increased but because our inventions have been cumulative.

Our consciousness has developed in the same way. A baby in today's world begins life with roughly the same mental equipment as its Cro-Magnon counterpart, but after a few years the difference is immense. All that we have learned in the intervening millennia—all the wisdom of language, culture, and science—flows into today's growing children from a thousand sources, so that by the time they are teenagers their sense of their place and potential in the world is radically different. Formal schooling finishes the job that acculturation, parenting, and environment began.

We shouldn't be too complacent about this accomplishment, though. Consciousness has not developed in a straight line. There may be areas—in their sensitivity to the harmonies of nature, for example—in which we have fallen behind our Cro-Magnon ancestors. They did not kill one another with the efficiency that we do, either. We still need, perhaps more than ever, that innate creativity that helps us survive and flourish in the world of our birth. Each generation's solutions leaves the next generation with new problems to solve.

For thousands of years we have been kings of invention, and the pace has been accelerating with each generation. But perhaps what we need now is not more invention, but less. Our incessant gadgeteering has brought us to the brink. Though most of our creativity has been well meaning, unintended consequences have multiplied. We also have to remember that the scheming of the criminal or the terrorist, the ingenuity of the tyrant, can be creative too.

We now need to apply all our creativity to slowing and even reversing this process, to return to the ancient ways of perception and understanding, to see the solution to nuclear waste, for example, not in building a better waste-processing plant but in finding in sun, water, and wind, nonpolluting sources of power.

This next step in the creative process will not occur in the realm of invention, nor in the outer world, but in the development of consciousness. So many of our inventions up to this point have been to satisfy various desires—the desire to be warm in winter and cool in summer—and, as Buddhism says in one of its vows, "desires are inexhaustible." We can continue to invent ingenious ways to satisfy our desires—this is the approach of the inventor—or we can change our consciousness so that we don't have so many of them. We need to find, as the Buddhist texts on right livelihood say, "fewness of wants and contentment."

This is not the task of Bell Research Laboratories; it is for us to do on our own. Each of us has this touch of magic. The bison cave paintings are testimony to this; so are the bow and arrow and the plow. Our brains are built for creation; we would never have survived without it. And within each of us is the four-year-old who can sweep his arm across the paper, crayon in hand, and say, "This is Mommy," and not notice or care that for someone else it is not. From that sweep of the arm everything can emerge, all that we need to enrich our lives and make them special. This is the higher purpose of the Creator's Work, to make us more fully human. Too many people forget the feeling of that sweep of the arm as they grow up, but it is always available to us.

This form of the Creator's Work can be understood in two ways. In the first, each of us is a Creator. In another way, the work does not belong to us at all, or to anyone. Every individual is a tiny piece of a vast creation, larger than himself or of any system or idea. We are all bound together in shared fate on one slow-moving island, which is the work space of all creation. This means that there is a connection between what we create in our minds, the kind of person we choose to be, the minds of others, and the island itself, the world in which we all live.

The Buddhists teach that in the depths of meditation we can intuitively experience this connection and shared creation, and understand that the whole world is a creation of Mind—not the personal individual mind, but the greater mind, Big Mind. This notion—called Mind-Only—would be puzzling to the mainstream of modern scientific thought, which sees only a material world obeying predetermined physical laws. But Buddhist thought is interested more in the subjective than the objective, in how we experience the world rather than the world by itself, in our relationship to a herd of bison rather than to the bison alone. In this way Buddhism is closer in sensibility to the paleolithic cave painters, who saw and painted the bison as kindred spirits, than to today's scientists. Some scientific research—particularly in the realm of medical healing—is beginning to explore the edges of this mind-body membrane, investigating, for example, whether visualization or prayer can affect the course of healing. But the worldview of Mind-Only goes beyond that; it posits that from the standpoint of consciousness, it is not the world that creates us, but we who create the world.

This means that the world we imagine is the one in which we are fated to live. This is why the Consciousness Project is not just a metaphor for progress. It is literal; what we imagine, individually and collectively, becomes our world. Imagine a weapon, and there it is. Imagine a song, and it sings to us. In our minds there are both destruction and creation, delusion and wisdom.

The choice between the two must accompany the basic creative act and become its indispensable companion. Otherwise the gift of creation goes astray, and turns dark. This destructive aspect of the Creator's Work comes from selfishness, greed, and pride. It is hasty and impatient, interested only in the craved result. In order to keep the gift of creation wholesome, we must cultivate its spiritual companion—patience.

Chapter 8

THE CREATOR'S CONSCIOUSNESS: PATIENCE

WE CANNOT MAKE a spark with flint or steel alone. We need both. Likewise, the Creator's Work needs two seemingly contradictory elements, which must combine in just the right way for the desired result: inspiration and patience.

Inspiration is hard to describe and even harder to define. Literally it means "breathing in." Like air, inspiration seems to come from outside; we cannot conjure it by force of will. Finding the creative spark is not like washing the dishes or mowing the lawn. You cannot simply sit down at your desk, stare at a blank canvas, or walk into your garage workshop and say to yourself, "Time to be creative!" The Creator's Work only half belongs to us; the other half is an alchemical mix of happenstance, gestation, and receptivity, which combine to produce a moment of inspiration or transformation. Artists, mathematicians, and scientists who depend on creativity have long realized that inspiration seems to arise at the very moment that willful effort recedes. "Eureka!" cried the Greek philosopher and inventor Archimedes as he was lowering himself into a bath. The solution to the problem that had been plaguing him for months—how to measure the volume of a solid object—had suddenly come to him.

Although inspiration arrives in its own time and way, it is intimately connected to what we do, and what we don't do. We must be patient, but not passive. We cannot be sitting in the railway station, waiting for a train. We need to be alert, attentive, and relaxed all at the same time—easier said than done. We might call this quality "pregnant receptivity." Something is there. We feel it, we know it is coming, but we can't force it. If we try, if we push on it before the right time, it doesn't help.

Writers have turned this insight into a running joke: "Time for another cup of tea!" they say. When the words don't come, there is always hope that an interlude in the kitchen fussing with the teakettle might unleash their creative juices. And they are not the only ones who create various rituals for producing this receptive state of mind. Baseball players on a hitting streak wear the same pair of socks for weeks on end; poets carry their notebooks wherever they go, never knowing when the Muse will strike. Norman Stiegelmeyer, a well-known West Coast painter, used to keep three radios going at the same time in his studio, "to keep my head clear," he said.

Inspiration and patience—one seemingly effortless, the other requiring effort. We know these two go together, but we don't know quite how. There are many books on the subject, instructing us in various methods to relax or "go with the flow." But those who know best—creative artists themselves—don't try to explain it. They just do it. "Being creative is just something we're all born with," says Naomi. "It's the essence of human experience."

∞

This interplay between patience and inspiration is also a feature of personal transformation and of the spiritual life. To "hit bottom," to be "born again," to be "enlightened," to become a "new person"—these epiphanies often come after a long period of expectation, struggle, even despair. In Buddhism, patience is one of the Paramitas, the primary virtues necessary for spiritual practice. Traditional Buddhist texts tend to define patience as the ability to put up with difficulty: "Patience means not to be fatigued by hardships, but to accept them joyfully"; "To be ready for everything without bothering about material considerations is the essence of patience." For Buddhist monks, living in voluntary poverty, this kind of forbearance was essential.

There is also in Buddhism an understanding of the connection between patience and inspiration, between suffering and enlightenment:

> The misery I have to endure in realizing
> Enlightenment is measurable:
> It is like probing a wound
> To stop the pain caused by what is lodged therein.

Shunryu Suzuki talked about patience too. But he did not use traditional Buddhists texts or terminology. Instead, he talked about frogs.

PATIENCE

Suzuki loved frogs. Even as a boy he seemed to have a natural sympathy for these creatures. In Suzuki's biography, *Crooked Cucumber,* by David Chadwick, is this story: "The young Suzuki overheard some older boys talking about going to a nearby creek and capturing and tormenting the frogs there. Suzuki quickly ran to the place and splashed all around, frightening all the frogs away so they would be safe from the older boys."

Once, in a lecture, Suzuki vividly imitated the way a frog waits for a meal. It sits utterly still, Suzuki said, demonstrating by showing us his most immobile meditation posture, until a little insect flies by and then—zap! Suzuki lunged forward on his meditation cushion, his tongue protruding, becoming, for the moment, a hungry frog snapping up the morsel on its long tongue. And then he laughed quietly to himself for what seemed a long time.

In *Not Always So,* Suzuki has this to say about frogs: "I always admire their practice. They never get sleepy. Their eyes are always open, and they do things intuitively in an appropriate way. When something to eat comes by, they go like this: GULP! They never miss anything, they are always calm and still. I wish I could be a frog."

Suzuki's frog story is charming, until we dig deeper and see the story from the point of view of the frog. The frog, motion-less and with full attention, is not performing a circus trick for our benefit, nor is it there as the subject of some spiritual homily. It is there because it is hungry. That is why it is willing to stay there until the fly comes along.

But when the fly does come—what happiness! All the wait-ing in the wind and the rain is redeemed at that moment. This is the breakthrough, the inspiration that makes the long wait worthwhile. The frog brings to life the dynamic tension between patience and inspiration, the connection between the waiting and the reward. Without the waiting there is no fly; but without the hope of a fly, why wait?

The point of Suzuki's story is to make the connection between the frog and each of us, to help us see that the frog's patience is connected with the inescapable conditions of the frog's life, with every creature's life, with our life. For the frog to get the fly it needs to cultivate two qualities. First, it must have unshakable confidence that the fly will eventually come. Without this confidence it will despair; how can it even go on living? The frog will wait forever, if necessary, in the hope of that fly.

The second quality it needs is alertness, tongue coiled and ready to strike, for as long as it takes for the fly to come. If the frog grows tired, if it decides to take a nap, it might miss the fly, and all the tedious waiting will have been for naught. If the frog goes away thinking, "Well, there will be no flies today," this relieves its tension, but leaves the frog no less hungry than when it began.

So the frog's patience, and our patience, is no ordinary waiting. It's hard work. And even if the fly comes, the work does not end. Soon the frog will again be hungry; the entire process will repeat itself, on and on. This is the frog's life, our life. This is Suzuki's point in telling us the story.

His story was also a lesson in how to do *zazen,* Zen meditation. The experience of *zazen* can be a sense of "nothing going on." Nothing is happening; we're just sitting there. We may not notice at first that this itself is something special. Where else can we have such an experience? Such practices are very old, and may have had their origins sometime in the Neolithic, when the daily life of prehistoric man and woman was connected with the slow rhythm of the sun and stars, the weather and the seasons.

In *The Real Work*, Gary Snyder says, "Our earlier ways of self-support, our earlier traditions of life prior to agriculture, required literally thousands of years of great attention and awareness, and long hours of stillness."

Zazen is not something unusual; if anything, it is the rest of our life that is unusual. And yet *zazen* is not just waiting, either. We think again of Suzuki's frog, sitting, waiting, seemingly doing nothing, until the insect buzzes by and the full energy of the frog's being suddenly comes to life as, in a flash, the insect is instantly transformed into a meal that contributes to the frog's survival. If this is meant to teach us about human life, then what is the lesson?

THE "NOT YET" MIND

Once, in a formal question-and-answer ceremony, a woman walked down between two rows of seated people to where Suzuki was sitting on a platform and said, *"Mada!"*

Suzuki sat up straight and said in a loud voice, "Yes! *Mada* is very important. *Mada* means *'not yet'*!"

Mada is Japanese for "not yet." Apparently Suzuki and the student had had a previous conversation about *mada,* and this interchange was the distillation of their encounters. On other occasions, Suzuki referred to the "Not Yet Mind," the mind that is content to wait—forever if necessary—for something to happen. What does this mean? How can an ordinary idea like "not yet" be so important?

When we are children, we understand that we are "not yet"

grown. When we are young, just out of college, we have the sense that we are "not yet" fully developed, our adult life and our career lie before us. As mature adults, with career and family, we look forward to growing old with a mixture of anticipation and dread; because it has "not yet" occurred, and yet is inevitable, we sense all the sadness and regret that come from the gradual passing away of our youthful ambitions and of those we love. And at the end of our years, there is impending death—one more "not yet."

Human beings are always caught up in some kind of "not yet." The slow, patient, sometimes boring time in *zazen* is also a kind of "not yet." From one point of view, our whole life is "not yet." And yet it is something more too. In every moment we are also arriving, we are already here, and the time has already come. This is the inspiration of each moment, which exists simultaneously with our waiting, with our sense of "not yet."

∞

If we think of the frog on its lily pad, waiting and watching for the cherished fly, we know that it is concentrating. It is not lazy or distracted. Its frog mind is in a state of heightened awareness. But what is the frog's actual situation? It is one with its hunger and its fate, having to endure cold rain and high wind, and if it has a mind to wonder, it thinks, Why this? Why me? Is there any escape from this situation? What can I do?

This is not just an effort to concentrate; it is a deeper quest, for meaning and for understanding. The frog is flooded with an urgent sense of "not yet." The fly has not yet come. The frog is still hungry. This is the moment when patience is most important. The frog must be open to whatever comes—hunger, fly, cold, heat, rain. If it is not prepared to just sit there forever, it cannot bear to stay on the lily pad long enough.

This is our human condition, too. We are always waiting for some kind of fly, always yearning, always tugging at the drawstrings of our circumstances for some way out. To continue on this path, to work forward day to day, week to week, looking for a way to edge closer to what we need and want, requires fortitude, a kind of patience or endurance.

There can be times when we are tempted to give up. But if we are fully engaged with our life, we do not. Amid the slogging, something happens, something unexpected, something outside the endless muddy track. This is the beginning, the first intimation, of the Creator's Work awakening in our hearts, perhaps akin to what John said in the last chapter: "I go to the place where music is and it comes to me."

This is the moment of inspiration and transformation, when something hits us and our life is changed. Rainer Maria Rilke described such a moment in his poem "Archaic Torso of Apollo." In a meditation on the beauty of an ancient Greek statue, he described it as "breaking out of all its contours/ Like a star: for there is no place/ that does not see you. You must change your life."

We must change our life. Something hits us and our life changes. These moments cannot be planned or predicted. They are inspired; they just come.

CHANGING YOUR LIFE

As I began to interview Phil for this book, I told him I was hoping to hear about his long career as a therapist specializing in group dynamics and conflict resolution.

"What's it *to* you?" he replied.

"I don't know," I said. "What do you mean?"

"Just like when you ask somebody on the street a question and he says, 'What's it to you?'"

I did the best I could to explain the purpose of the book and why I wanted to talk to him.

Phil wasn't just being ornery. But he didn't want to just *do* an interview. If he was going to reveal the details of his life to me, he wanted me to reveal the details of mine to him—my purpose, my motivation, my mission. Phil was well known and admired for his plain-talking style. It was only when he proceeded to tell me his life story that I understood why.

"I grew up in Iowa," he said, "and before I was out of high school I was working in a meatpacking plant. I was a good knife guy in the plant; a good cleanup guy."

He went on to tell me about his troubles as a young adult, his slow descent into alcoholism, and his introduction to Alcoholics Anonymous by an older man named Jack.

"Jack was the toughest guy I'd ever met," said Phil. "He'd seen it all, and you couldn't put anything past him. I was in rotten shape, and feeling pretty sorry for myself. I didn't think this AA nonsense could do a damn thing for me, and I thought probably Jack didn't think so either.

"Then, after several meetings he walked up to me, unbuttoned his shirt, pointed to his nipple, and said, 'You know, kid, I understand you. You're the kind of guy that's going to need to be wet-nursed, and that's fine, I'm happy to do it, but you're going to have to get close. All I got is these little bitty tits.'

"My whole life just turned around right then," Phil said. "I can't say why, exactly, but somehow Jack got to me in a way that no one else had. When he said that, something just opened up for me."

Phil soon became an AA group leader himself, and not long after that, he found himself forging relationships with some of the leading lights of the human potential movement. Before long he was enrolled in a postgraduate university seminar for training specialists in group therapy—he, a high school dropout.

True inspiration, the kind that turns our life around, doesn't come cheap. The inspired moment that changes our life—the fly that suddenly appears before the frog—cannot be predicted. But it comes, and Phil's life story is a testament to its power. Without Patience—or in Phil's case, a kind of dogged desperation—the fly will come and go and we will never see it, and wonder, waiting on our wilting lily pad, when the life we want or imagine will ever begin.

PATIENCE AND THE
CONSCIOUSNESS PROJECT

Patience is a difficult virtue to come by in our fast-paced, wired world. These days we wait for nothing. If we wish to call our home or office we merely reach for our cell phone. If we want to find out what is happening halfway across the world, a click of the television remote satisfies us. Researchers who study how children learn know that preschoolers who watch children's TV shows, with their puppet-led instruction in the A-B-Cs, tend to be less imaginative in creating their own games— the so-called *Sesame Street* syndrome. Presumably, they depend on such shows to provide their creativity for them. The pace and machinery of modern civilization compresses their experience of time, removes their chance to experience a state of "nothing going on," and stultifies the creative nerve centers of their brains.

If the creative, transformative moment is mysterious when it occurs in an individual, how much more so is the cultural evolution that occurs when all the individuals in each generation pool their respective eurekas. How rare it is these days for people to think much beyond their own life spans, to the welfare of their grandchildren's children or the landscape or the planet. When is the last time you heard anyone speak of a hundred- or five-hundred-year plan? And yet there are carpenters in England who can point to specific oak trees and know from old manuscripts that they were planted five hundred years earlier to replace roof beams in historical buildings.

The Consciousness Project has a time horizon even vaster. In its pursuit we must think not in hundreds but in thousands of years, and who has the luxury to do that when the exigencies of daily life are so engrossing? And yet some of us must, if there is to be any hope for the long term. "Life is short; art is long," said Hippocrates. And, we might add, consciousness is even longer. We hope we will be here a thousand, ten thousand years from now, but how much do we really think about it?

We think about the grim alternative even less. There is a Zen koan: "When the universal fire destroys everything, what then?" Little did the author of this saying know that one day the universal fire would be real, a frightful bomb, another well-meaning invention of man the gadgeteer, and that it can indeed consume everything. And so we too must ask ourselves, "What then?" from the viewpoint of someone inside the problem. "What then? What can we do?"

QUESTIONS TO ASK, THINGS TO DO

Waiting

Mel, a fellow disciple of Shunryu Suzuki, now seventy-two and longtime leader of his own Buddhist group, recently said, "Everything important has come to me through waiting." Mel is well known for his patience. And yet he did not share this revelation with me as though it had come to him easily.

You can test Mel's understanding for yourself. Pick an area of your life that has been chronically frustrating, that has defeated all your efforts to solve. Perhaps it is a bad situation at work, a difficult relationship, a financial worry. Undoubtedly you believe you have tried everything. But have you tried waiting with full attention? Have you allowed yourself to be like the frog on the lily pad? Is it possible that if you did, something unexpected would happen, something beyond your understanding or plans?

Ryokan, the Zen monk quoted earlier, knew something about waiting. He lived alone in a broken-down cottage, a hermit who spent his days writing poetry and playing ball with children. One day his brother asked him to come to his house and do something for his delinquent son. "Ryokan came as asked. [But though his brother waited and waited all day and into the night], Ryokan did not say a word of admonition to the boy. He stayed overnight and prepared to leave the next morning. As the wayward nephew was lacing Ryokan's straw sandals, he felt a warm drop of water. Glancing up, he saw Ryokan looking down at him, his eyes full of tears. Ryokan then returned home, and the nephew changed for the better."

Ryokan, it seems, didn't know what to do in that situation any more than most people would. But unlike most people, he didn't force the issue. He didn't fill up the day with well-meaning remarks. It wasn't until the end of his visit that the time came: the moment of his departure, looking down at the nephew lacing up his sandals. Ryokan didn't *try* to cry. The nephew didn't expect to change.

But they saw each other and the feeling came to them both, a mutual inspiration. As Rilke said, "You must change your life."

Chapter 9

THE MONK'S WORK

❧

THE GREEK ROOT of the English word *monk* means "alone." Whether monks live in communities or by themselves, solitude is their defining characteristic. Monks, of whatever order or faith, are people who confront their fundamental aloneness. That is what makes them special. Professional monks focus on this work their entire lives, but all of us can do it. In fact, we *need* to do it, in some fashion that fits our life station, because we each need to face this fundamental aloneness at some time in our lives if we are to be complete. This is not just a specialty of religious professionals; it is our human condition.

This confrontation with our fundamental aloneness can take different forms as we go through life. When we are children we approach solitude, as we do every experience, in the spirit of curiosity and play. Children will lie on their backs and watch the clouds passing in the sky with no sense of purpose or time.

If an adult happens by and asks, "What are you doing?" the child will just shrug and run off to some other game, not realizing that in some spiritual traditions, sky gazing is a profound exercise in self-awareness.

Late adolescence and early adulthood is the time when this intimation of aloneness—an inner "me"—is most powerful. Young adults respond to this intimation either by spending as much time as possible with their friends—fending off the challenge of solitude—or by isolating themselves, fiercely embracing their aloneness. This is a challenging time of life. Young adults often become depressed, even suicidal, as they struggle to establish their sense of individual identity in a society that has lost many of its spiritual and communal moorings.

As we move through early and middle adulthood this intimation of solitude often recedes, while we concentrate on making our way in the world and building a career. But as we approach middle age it tends to surface again, in midlife crisis, when we confront divorce, illness, regret, and a growing sense of mortality. In old age, the Monk's Work rises again with even more force, as we reflect on the life we have lived and the end that is to come.

We may lead complicated and busy lives, but throughout our life the inner monk is our hidden companion, always watching and waiting for an opportunity to rise and be heard.

TRADITIONAL FORMS OF MONK'S WORK

Nearly all traditional cultures acknowledge some form of the Monk's Work and provide ways to cultivate and express it. In Native American cultures entry into adulthood was often marked by a period of solitude, when young adults would go alone into the wilderness to seek a vision or song to give them strength. In Southeast Asia, it was common to send high school boys to local monasteries for training in meditation. Ancient Hinduism held that the best time for the Monk's Work was later in life. Its doctrine envisioned human life in four stages: the student, the householder, the hermitage dweller, and finally the full renunciate, seeking wisdom in solitude.

Partly because our modern world lacks these forms of inner inquiry and initiation, traditions such as Buddhism have become popular in the West, leading to the development of retreat centers throughout the United States—twenty-five such centers in the Catskills region of New York alone. In such places a person can pursue meditation for weeks, months, or even years, in a modern re-creation of traditional Monk's Work that would have been hard to imagine in this country a few decades ago.

The story of Richard, age thirty-five, illustrates how these retreat centers can function effectively in a person's life. A magazine editor, Richard used his accumulated vacation days to attend a ten-day retreat led by James, a teacher in the Vipassana tradition of Buddhist meditation. Richard had been studying with James for some time and considered him his spiritual mentor.

Richard had been under a lot of stress lately. His employer was in trouble financially; there were rumors of impending layoffs. His father had recently died after a long struggle with cancer, and his girlfriend of three years had been talking about reassessing their relationship. So, when the retreat began, Richard brought several burdens to his meditation cushion. He was hoping that, as in previous retreats, meditation could provide him some respite from his troubles.

However, to his dismay, calm proved elusive. Instead, as the retreat entered its second day he felt powerful waves of anxiety and fear. He arranged an appointment with James to discuss this unexpected development.

"What am I doing wrong?" he asked James as soon as he sat down in the interview room. "I'm more anxious than when I got here!"

After asking him what was going on in his life, James realized that Richard had come to the retreat in a state of personal crisis. "The purpose of meditation is not just to attain a calm state of mind," James explained. "It's about paying attention to everything that is going on, pleasant or unpleasant. Sometimes our mind is busy, sometimes quiet, sometimes calm, sometimes anxious. You've brought a lot of problems with you to this retreat. Your main job is to create a space to contain them."

"I don't know," Richard sighed. "I was hoping to get away from all my worries for a few days."

James smiled. "I used to think that way too, when I was studying in Burma. But my teacher just laughed when I told him that, and reminded me that meditation is hard work. Your worries are real enough, but the best way to work on them is to be conscious of them without trying to resolve them just now."

Richard returned to his meditation cushion and for the next eight days tried to follow James's advice. It was very difficult, but on the last day, his mental anguish cleared, and he was able to abide in a deep inner calm.

Richard did not lose his job. However, his girlfriend did decide to end their relationship. That caused Richard much grief, but he found solace in recollecting the deep calm he had achieved during the retreat.

If anyone were to think that this kind of work is not "real" work, Richard would be able to set him straight. "Those ten days were just about the hardest in my life," he said. "Some days my clothes were soaked, I was sweating so much." Richard's problems were about his relationships in the outer world: his job, his father, his girlfriend. We might think that the solution to these problems would also be in the outside world. We might want Richard to talk to a grief counselor about his father, to be proactive about his employment situation, to go into couples therapy with his girlfriend. These might have given him symptomatic relief, but instead through meditation he went deep within, finally reaching a place of calm that helped him in a much more fundamental way. He did the Monk's Work.

MODERN FORMS OF MONK'S WORK

We think of monks in their cowls and robes as carriers of an ancient tradition, and the ones alive today as vestiges of that tradition. But the Monk's Work didn't end with the Middle Ages. It has just taken different forms. Two common forms of the Monk's Work today are psychotherapy and prayer. One originates in the secular, the other in the religious sphere, but both are introspective in nature. In both cases we look not without but within. Of course, there are differences. Therapy is conducted in partnership with a trained professional, while prayer, even in a congregation, is essentially private. The end result—personal solace and transformation—is similar.

This was certainly true for Bryan, who sought the help of a psychiatrist after a stint working for an abusive boss. After being summarily fired, Bryan was overwhelmed with anger and self-doubt. He thought his dismissal was unjustified and felt shattered by the abuse and criticism he'd endured at the hands of his superior. Over a period of months, Bryan's doctor helped him realize that he had had a lifelong pattern of subordinating himself to powerful men. The doctor was skillful enough never to point this out directly. Bryan was able to make the connection himself, an insight that gave him the confidence to break that old pattern. Soon his depression had lifted and he had started his own business.

Was Bryan's transformation an instance of the Monk's Work? There was nothing traditionally monklike about it; in fact, during this time he also pursued a passionate love affair. And how could an hour a week at the psychiatrist's office qualify as work? But Bryan explained to me that during this period in his life, while he lived off his savings, he spent many hours mulling over the issues that surfaced during his weekly therapy session. Inside he was hard at work. The result of his effort was as real as any financial reward.

Prayer can be deeply transforming too, as Anna's story shows. When her seven-year-old daughter was diagnosed with a life-threatening but potentially curable form of leukemia, Anna coped with the crisis with periods of concentrated prayer, drawing on her religious upbringing as an observant Jew. With guidance from her rabbi, she developed the faith to help her daughter endure several months of debilitating chemotherapy. On leave from her job as a social worker, dealing with her daughter's cancer became Anna's main work. She emerged from this period of crisis stronger and more resourceful as a person. She also discovered, as she returned to her job as a social worker, that she was able to bring new depth and compassion to her work. Doing the Monk's Work on behalf of her daughter changed her life.

NONTRADITIONAL FORMS OF MONK'S WORK

Jeanine arrived at her desk one morning at the software company where she worked and found a pink slip waiting for her. Her first reaction was panic. Find another job, any job, she thought. But after a few days' scouring the want ads, she became exhausted. So she loaded her backpack and drove from her Manhattan apartment to hike part of the Appalachian Trail.

She spent two weeks in the forest, walking the ridgelines from southern New York into New Jersey. She had no conscious notion of doing the Monk's Work. She was just following her instinct to get away. During this time she took stock of her feelings and aspirations. By the time she emerged from the wilderness, she had decided that the pink slip was not really the disaster she had thought, but a message and an opportunity. She realized that she had never liked her job anyway. Here was a chance to combine her computer skills with her lifelong interest in art and pursue a career in computer-aided graphic design. She attended some classes and soon landed a good job in her newfound vocation.

Jeanine's expression of the Monk's Work was different from Anna's, but the result was the same—her life changed, and for the better.

HEALING AS MONK'S WORK

Sometimes, due to accident or illness, we find ourselves doing the Monk's Work involuntarily. That was my experience. In July 1999, while juggling three careers—as software entrepreneur, author and Buddhist lecturer, and musician/composer—I was struck down by a severe case of viral encephalitis. I was in a coma for ten days and nearly died. I awoke to discover that I had sustained major neurological damage and would need two years of painstaking rehabilitation and healing to recover.

The Monk's Work had been my full-time profession for fifteen years—I was an ordained Buddhist priest and meditation teacher in the Zen Buddhist tradition—but I soon discovered that all my meditation training had only limited applicability in dealing with the aftereffects of this illness. Meditation requires a functional brain, but my illness had scrambled many of my neurological circuits. My vision and hearing were distorted, my body had too much adrenaline, and my attention span was only about ten minutes.

After more than four years I have fully recovered, but the experience was deeply humbling. I experienced my vulnerability and my fear of dying. I began to understand the way my intellect often obscured my empathy for others. Gradually I realized that this terrible illness was also a gift. For nearly a year my recovery was my full-time job. I was even "paid" for it— with disability insurance! I had worked hard all my life, but never as hard as I did that year.

During my recovery, one of my therapists told me about her nephew who had broken both legs in a ski accident and was confined to a hospital bed in a full body cast for nearly a year. In the accounts of my illness she heard echoes of her nephew's experience. An avid skier and athlete, he lay in bed week after week, in as much mental as physical agony, wondering, Will I ever ski again? Will I ever *walk* again? What is to become of me? What kind of future does life hold for me?

The nephew would undoubtedly be amazed to hear that he was doing a form of the Monk's Work. There was nothing in his outward circumstance as an immobilized hospital patient that resembled any traditional picture we might have of a monk. Nor was his state of mind at all calm; in fact, he was filled with foreboding and despair. But there was one way in which he was indeed a working "monk": He was, involuntarily and most painfully, alone with his mind. He could not move, and could watch television, read magazines, or receive visitors, for only so many hours a day. The rest of the time he had no choice but to grapple with the inner crisis enveloping his life. He was facing not just the fundamental aloneness that all of us must one day face but the possibility that his future life might be severely compromised.

My therapist ended her story with the news that her nephew was now not only walking but was back on the ski slopes with a sense of gratitude and appreciation for his recovery. As painful as it was, his year in the hospital, doing the Monk's Work, had changed his life.

∞

These examples illustrate our universal human need to cultivate the inner life of solitude. Though our modern world may have lost touch with this need and the cultural forms that once existed to fill it, the Monk's Work remains necessary if we are to live satisfying and meaningful lives. We don't need it always; there may be times when it recedes in favor of other kinds of work. But like an essential vitamin or mineral, it is a nutrient that we cannot do without for long.

Whether we tarry in the world of the Monk's Work only when we are in crisis, like many of the examples presented above, or manage to integrate it into the ebb and flow of our daily life, the Monk's Work helps us to know who we are, and as we come to the end of our life, to feel satisfied with what we have done and who we have become.

Paradoxically, though solitude defines the Monk's Work and gives it its power, it benefits not only ourselves but others—our friends, our families, even the larger society. We see this dynamic reflected in the social structure of medieval Europe, for example, when the Monk's Work was honored as a lifelong vocation for those called to it, and the monasteries were centers of learning and exemplars of spiritual wisdom for the whole society.

Today in most parts of the world the monastery has receded as a central social institution, but our need for the Monk's Work may be the driving force behind the creation of a new kind of monastery, one that is neither separate from the world nor a sanctuary for lifelong renunciates, but a place where all of us can come and go, a cloister of spiritual nourishment and safety that gives us a chance to find shelter and respite from our outer life.

Chapter 10

THE MONK'S CONSCIOUSNESS: CALM

෨

THE SPIRITUAL PRACTICE that supports and enriches the Monk's Work is Calm. Calm, once an integral part of daily life, has been somewhat neglected in our outwardly focused modern world. But still we seek it. We stop for a moment to enjoy a sunset, or enjoy the serenity of walking by the lake in a park. But for most people these experiences are transitory, notwithstanding the fact that whole spiritual traditions have been built around them.

Those schooled in Buddhist doctrine know that the old texts distinguish calm, or *samattha,* from insight, *vipassana.* It is frequently pointed out that Gautama the Buddha, though adept in deep trance states, achieved enlightenment not while in trance but in a more ordinary state of mind, when he opened his eyes and saw the morning star rising. Some think that to describe the Monk's Work as only about calm is one-sided; the Monk's work, they say, should include both calm and insight. Gautama,. they say, was a consummate master in all the states of *samattha,* but it was not until he opened his eyes, literally and figuratively, that wisdom dawned.

This story illustrates the usual notion of Calm as a precursor to insight. However, these distinctions are somewhat artificial. Calm and insight are not two things; they arise together. A calm mind is one that can see into the real nature of things. A mind that sees this way—a mind of wisdom—is intrinsically calm. (See chapter 18 for more about wisdom.) For now let us simply recognize that Calm is the gate to the Monk's Work. Once inside this garden of repose, this work space of our fundamental aloneness, the various flowers of insight can begin to open.

CALM AND SITTING

In the late 1960s, the first Zen monastery in America was founded at Tassajara, an old hot-springs resort in the Big Sur mountains of California. One day Hans, a young Swedish carpenter whose imperfect command of English was further affected by several beers, showed up at the monastery gate.

"Why are you here?" the monastery director asked him.

"I want to study Zen!" Hans replied in a loud voice.

"Have you ever sat?" the director continued, using "sat" as monastery shorthand for *zazen,* or Zen meditation.

Hans frowned in confusion. He understood the meaning of the English words but could not fathom why he was being asked such a simpleminded question. Was the director making fun of him? Was this a Zen trick? If so, he was not about to be fooled. Finally he drew himself up and said forcefully, "All people have sat!"

Of course Hans was right, and perhaps only a non-native speaker would have missed the nuance of the director's question. The physical act of sitting is obviously something we do all the time, a minute here, a minute there. In that sense, there is some superficial similarity between quietly sitting on our living room sofa and the "just sitting" of *zazen*. The difference lies in our attention and our intention. Sitting on our sofa, our attention is focused on whatever we are doing—reading the newspaper, watching television, chatting with a companion. In *zazen*, our attention is focused on the sitting itself—on our posture, our breathing, and our state of mind. It is hard to say what our intention is on the sofa; it could be anything—probably just to relax and be comfortable. But in *zazen*, our intention is do what Gautama did: achieve a calm state of mind and seek insight about ourselves. Sitting on the sofa to relax is not Monk's Work, but sitting on our meditation cushion is.

When the director asked Hans, "Have you ever sat?" for a moment he may have forgotten that he was speaking to a newcomer. What he really meant was, "Have you ever done *zazen*—have you ever sat down and faced your fundamental aloneness?" For that is the essence of *zazen*, and of the Monk's Work—this fundamental aloneness that, through long study, may turn into a fundamental oneness and connectedness. It is work that no one can do for us, but if we fail to do it at all, over time we may be misled by external conditions, until some life crisis wakes us up and we realize that we have neglected an essential part of our well-being: taking the time to really *sit*, not just on our living room sofa but in the arena of our meditation cushion and one's own mind.

The monastery director probably could have communicated

this more clearly to Hans. As for Hans, it might have helped if he had come to the monastery gate sober. Nevertheless, the upshot of the story was that Hans entered the monastery as a student, learned to sit *zazen,* and stayed for many years, eventually becoming someone who could ask another newcomer, "Have *you* ever sat?"

CALM AND BREATHING

The director might also have asked Hans, "Have you ever breathed?" Hans would have found that question equally silly. Of course we have all breathed. We breathe about 36,000 times a day, 13 million times a year. It is astonishing how little we pay attention to this ever-present function, which, next to our heartbeat, is the most precious to us. Only when we are quiet and attentive do we notice it.

But why notice it at all? What could be at all interesting about something as plain and primitive as breathing? Language gives us one answer. The English word *spirit* comes from the Latin word *spiritus,* meaning "breath." Many religious traditions have connected the breath with spiritual life and the soul, and have taught that paying attention to the breath is a gate to that realm.

So, unlike other kinds of work, the Monk's Work is soul work, and one of the many ways to engage in it is to sit quietly and attend to the breath. This notion, thirty years ago so exotic in the West, has become commonplace. Many people are now familiar with meditation on the breath. It is no longer a mystery. In any case, the real mystery lies in ourselves. Attending to the breath opens the door to that mystery, and allows what is in the depths of ourselves to rise to the surface, like bubbles from the bottom of the ocean.

The work lies in dealing with the bubbles. In each of the case studies in the preceding chapter, the person had an encounter with one of these "bubbles." Only for Richard did this happen during meditation. For the others it was some life crisis, a crack in the smooth sidewalk of everyday life.

The breath is a doorway. It opens a space so our inner life can come forth from the shadows and into the light, to be seen and heard. As all the people in the last chapter can testify, meeting with these aspects of our inner drama is no picnic; it is hard work, the Monk's Work. Remember Jeanine, whose first reaction when she lost her job was immediately to seek another. Luckily, her deeper self redirected her. She went walking, an activity that is another gate to our inner world.

CALM AND WALKING

In *Work as a Spiritual Practice,* I pointed out the obvious: No matter what our jobs, whether in an office or on a construction site, we walk, even if only to the copy machine or the bathroom. Is that walking time wasted, or is it an opportunity? The Buddha taught the doctrine of the four postures: walking, standing, sitting, lying down. If we consider this teaching, we realize that it covers our whole life.

We may not notice that we breathe, but it is hard to avoid noticing that we walk. And that very noticing can change our mental state. When jogging first came into vogue, many years ago, its practitioners spoke of the "runner's high," that feeling of elation that takes hold as we lope through space.

Why was Jeanine's walk through the Appalachian woods a life-changing event? Would she have had the same insights if she had stayed home in her Manhattan apartment? How important were the scenes of nature that surrounded her? As she strolled along, wondering what to do with her life, did she think, "I am hard at work here"?

Walking is of course a kind of physical work. But what kind of mental work are we doing as well? Just our usual inner dialogue? Are we having a conversation on our cell phone? Idly speculating about the people on the sidewalk passing us by? Or are we attending to the very act of walking itself, and saying to ourselves, as Buddhist monks have done for centuries, "Now I am walking." And is there a tinge of wonder in that realization, as we recognize that there is something miraculous about it—amazing that we are here at all!

If that is our attitude, then walking has become Monk's Work, and we can be like Jeanine, who came back into the world with not only an empty backpack but a soul cleansed and a mind open to hitherto unglimpsed opportunities.

"All people have walked!" This too is true. But how many walk like Jeanine did, like the Buddhist monks of old did, like the Christian monks whose pilgrimages took them across Europe, in whose landscape they saw the hand of God? Walking is itself holy, as are all the simplest things of life, and in it we can find the Monk's Work even if it is only a stroll down the boulevard at lunchtime in the sunshine. If the gate to our soul is open, whether this detour into the Monk's Work is months or years, or just a few minutes, is not the critical issue.

OTHER GATES TO CALM

So far we have discussed traditional, spiritually oriented methods of cultivating Calm. But we have also seen that the Monk's Work, like eating or sleeping, satisfies a basic human need, and we have an intuitive sense of this, whether we are spiritually inclined or not. And many activities that are usually considered merely recreational also have a quality of the Monk's Work.

Consider fishing. This popular recreation might appear at first to have little to do with Calm, as its purpose is recreational—and to catch fish. But talk to any fisherman or -woman and we discover that the matter is more complex. Listen to them speak about how relaxed they feel in their small boat looking out on a lake's still waters, or the way life's worries seem to recede in a larger communion with nature. They may even admit that they throw the fish back, for it is not the capture that counts, but the thrill they feel when the fish takes the hook.

Of course, as with sitting or breathing, there is real fishing and there is sitting in a boat with a fishing pole. A boisterous beer party on a roaring motorboat is not quite Calm. But when fishing becomes a vehicle for a deeper meeting of mind and great nature, it can verge on the spiritual.

INTENTION

Conscious intention is one of our most powerful inner resources. When we pray, intention is the faculty that determines whether to pray for a winning lottery ticket or the welfare of our loved ones. Intention determines whether, when we sit down in our living room chair, we pick up the remote and flip on the TV, or let ourselves remain for a while in silence. Intention is an inner compass that orients us in soul space.

It is also the key to Calm, because, as Richard discovered in the preceding chapter, at first Calm can be anything but calm. Before calm comes we need to say to ourselves, "Whatever happens, I will face what lies within me." That thought is itself calming, as the eye of the storm is calm.

Consider the case studies in the last chapter. Each of them, in his or her way, began the Monk's Work with an act of resolve, of intent. Anna determined to pray; Richard decided to attend James's retreat; Bryan made his first appointment to see a psychiatrist; Jeanine packed her bag and went on a walk. These decisions are rarely easy. They can be like pushing back a heavy iron gate, thick with rust, to enter a hidden garden. Often the garden is hidden because it can be painful to go there. But intention redeems us. Intention makes us push the gate, or pick up the phone, or pack our bags.

In the end, intention is a quality that makes us fully human.

CALM AND SCIENCE

As meditation has become more commonplace, science has begun to take an interest. We are coming to understand that Calm is not just a fad but a serious discipline validated by experimental science. Just as we now know that alcoholism is not a character flaw but a disease with an organic and genetic basis, and that depression is not some divine punishment but an imbalance of neurotransmitters, we now know that Calm is state of mind that is scientifically measurable. Just as anxiety changes blood pressure, heart rate, and electrical conductivity of the skin—the basis for biofeedback—Calm produces measurable changes in brain activity.

It is not yet clear what this really means, except to tell us that what happens during periods of Calm is not just wishful thinking; it is real. The Monk's Work produces a change in how our brain functions just as the physical work of swinging a sledgehammer makes us sweat. Neurologists are far from being able to tell us why, for example, Jeanine's sojourn on the Appalachian Trail gave her the clarity to make an important life decision, but they can confirm that there is something more to it than happenstance. It may be that over time we will conclude that so-called theoneurology can't really explain how Calm helps our lives, any more than measuring Michael Jordan's muscle tone explains why he can sink a thirty-foot jump shot. But it can reassure the skeptical that Calm is real, as are its benefits.

THE MONK'S WORK AND THE CONSCIOUSNESS PROJECT

Solitude is indeed the defining characteristic of the Monk's life. The examples of the last chapter showed people in various forms of personal crisis, and for most people that is the condition that impels us to seek the Monk's Work and the Calm that accompanies it. But more broadly, we should not wait until crisis forces us, just as we should not wait until we suddenly become unemployed to plan our future careers. The best way to practice the Monk's Work is to do it regularly, whether we think we need to or not. Just as we shouldn't wait until we have a heart attack to maintain a program of regular physical exercise, we should not wait until we are faced with a life crisis to turn our attention inward.

The Consciousness Project—both our personal one and the collective one—cannot proceed only in the realm of activity. It is not just a program for universal human betterment—although it includes that. The great work of helping people—beginning with ourselves—must derive its basic sustenance from the realm of Calm, from fundamental solitude. Otherwise our outward activity, however beneficent it may seem, will tend to go awry. *Doing* needs to alternate with *being,* periods of doing with periods of nondoing. Like the work of raising a heavy ship's anchor, there needs to be some rhythm to the process—activity, reflection, doing, being.

It is true that at present our overly busy culture may seem to provide little encouragement for this sort of alternation, but do we allow our culture to define how we live our life, or do we realize that how we live our life also defines the culture? Our society is nothing more than the sum total of the lives of everyone in it. As more and more people discover the importance of Calm to a life well lived, our culture will change, in ways we might find hard to imagine.

To quote T. S. Eliot, Calm is the "still point of the turning world." It is also the still point of our turning life. To take the thought further: Without paying close attention to the still point, it is difficult to turn our life effectively. The two go together.

QUESTIONS TO ASK, THINGS TO DO

Sitting and Breathing

By now the basic Buddhist instructions for sitting and following the breath are quite familiar to many Americans. But it never hurts to repeat them. Go to a quiet place. Sit in a chair or cross-legged on the floor. Fold your hands in your lap. Adjust your posture so that you are leaning neither right nor left, and your spine is straight. Let your eyes half close, and gradually, without forcing, let your attention come to rest in the rise and fall of your breath. It may help to concentrate on the movement in your chest and abdomen, or on the subtle sensation of the air flowing in and out through your nostrils.

Next—and for many this is the most difficult part—don't try to *do* anything. Let the thinking and feeling that fills your mind slowly wind down, while you keep your attention lightly centered on your breath. Let your breath be the calm center of the mind's spinning top. Eventually you may enter a state that is neither ordinary wakefulness nor sleep but something altogether different—the state of Calm, or *samattha*.

In this state, the mind's deeper wisdom—usually concealed by ordinary activity—can begin to come out. As it does, try to suspend judgment. Don't label what happens as good or bad. Be content to enjoy a kind of mental democracy, in which all thoughts are created equal. This is the basic entry point of Calm. It sounds so simple; but a lifetime of practice will not exhaust its potential. Through its portal your whole life can flow. Through its filter your whole mind can be purified.

How long should you abide in this condition? A student once asked Shunryu Suzuki if five minutes was enough. "Why not ten minutes?" Suzuki replied. "Or twenty? That may be better." Another student complained, "I think your forty-minute meditation periods are too long. Why can't we stop at thirty?" Suzuki laughed and replied, "Actually, I was thinking of extending it to fifty minutes, but I'll meet you halfway. We'll do forty."

In other words, do what you can.

Walking

Again, find a quiet place, perhaps a sandy beach, a forest trail, or even the sidewalk of a quiet street. As you begin to walk, attend not to the thoughts that fill your mind but on the sensation of walking itself. Feel the soles of your feet as they touch the ground. Sense the swinging of your arms, the alternating rhythm of your legs. In other words, consciously focus your attention on what you are doing—walking. This ability to direct our attention wherever we choose is the secret of all spiritual practice; it is what distinguishes meditation from loneliness.

Instead of being intimidated by solitude, we embrace it, understanding that the mind, just as it is, is our treasure. It is also our responsibility. There is much in this uncertain world we cannot control, but at least our mind is our own. In this way Calm can be cultivated amid activity and, over time, extended to other, more complex activities.

Fishing

Fishing in this sense is not necessarily literal fishing. For some people, "fishing" may take the form of sitting in a room while quiet music plays. For others, "fishing" might be jogging, or driving, or knitting. The point is to recognize that in the course of our day, or week, there are many opportunities for Calm. Calm is indeed a kind of fishing expedition into the deep waters of the mind. Some days we may land a big fish, other days none at all. It is not catching the fish that defines Calm, but the waiting, the attention, and the firm resolve.

In Calm, we become a fisherman of the mind, an angler of the soul. Who knows what might be swimming just below the surface, waiting to seize the hook?

Chapter 11

THE HELPER'S WORK

❧

MAXIMILIAN KOLBE was a Catholic priest in Poland during World War II. Swept up by the tides of war, he was imprisoned in the Auschwitz concentration camp. Food was scarce. At the end of each workday the prisoners rushed to get their bits of bread, but Father Kolbe always waited until last, and often did not eat at all. After the others had gone to bed, he went from bunk to bunk saying, "I am a Catholic priest. Can I do anything for you?"

One day in July 1941 a man from Kolbe's group escaped. In order to discourage escapes, there was a rule that if a man got away, ten men would be killed in retaliation. When the fugitive was not found, the commandant gathered the prisoners together and told them that ten would be locked in a bunker without food or water until they died.

One of the ten could not help crying out in anguish, fearing what would happen to his wife and children. At that moment Father Kolbe stepped forward and said to the commandant, "Take me instead."

The commandant was astonished. "What?" he said.

Kolbe explained again that he was a Catholic priest, and wanted to take the other man's place because the man had a family.

⌒∞⌒

This story of personal sacrifice—made not for family or child, not for country or religious zealotry or fame, but simply to help another human being, a stranger—can be understood and appreciated by everyone. The question, How can I help this person? might occur to any of us. What we find extraordinary is Father Kolbe's answer, which led him to make the ultimate sacrifice. We think to ourselves, "How incredible! What courage! I would never have courage like that." But from the stories of victims of the September 11, 2001, terrorist attacks, the accounts of people who stayed behind in the burning buildings to help those who were disabled or blind, the actions of the people on the airplanes that crashed, we know that in the most extreme circumstances ordinary people can also rise to this standard of selflessness.

This willingness to help another person is too basic to be simply something we learn. Certainly children learn as they grow that the welfare of others is important. But the fundamental urge to reach out and help is etched in our souls. Sometimes this impulse is trivial, as when we motion to a less-burdened shopper to go ahead of us in the checkout line; sometimes, as in the case of Father Kolbe, it transcends life itself.

Even animals can exhibit this capacity. Jeffrey Masson, in

his book *Unconditional Love of Dogs,* tells the following tale, which was originally published in an 1842 book called *Animal Biography:* "A young man took a dog into a boat, rowed to the center of the Seine, and threw the animal over, with intent to drown him. The poor dog often tried to climb up the side of the boat; his master as often pushed him back, till, over-balancing himself, he fell overboard. As soon as the faithful dog saw his master in the stream, he left the boat and held him above water until help arrived from the shore, and his life was saved."

Some might say the animal didn't realize it was being drowned, and helped its master through blind loyalty. But we sense that this isn't quite true. Do we really think that the dog didn't know it was being abused? There is something in the dog's action that moves us. We exclaim, "That's so human!" Actually, it's more than human. How many of us could forgive to that degree?

This is the Helper's Work—not just an abstraction, not a personality trait to be parsed and calculated by ethical theorists. It is real work, work that our soul needs us to do to be whole: mentoring our colleagues at work, helping our friends move, joining our neighbors to clear out a clogged drainpipe or raise the barn roof, pitching in to build the flood wall, cooperating to thresh the wheat, to plant the rice. This quality is essential both for society and for ourselves. Without it we and others would be so alone. Helping supports us and keeps us afloat in a network of shared fate and reciprocal feeling.

SOMEONE TO HELP US

Phil, whom we met in chapter 8, wears a prosthesis on his left leg and had this story to tell about helping. One day, as he was leaving the hospital after a visit, his prosthesis suddenly snapped, and he went sprawling in the lobby.

"I was flat on my face when this guy shows up," Phil told me.

"He reached down to help me up. 'You all right?'

"'Yeah,' I said. 'I'm all right.'

"'You want me to call a doctor?'

"That's the last thing I wanted. 'No, just help me get out of here.'

"I took out twenty bucks and my car keys and said, 'I got a Mustang in the parking garage, it's got a handicap license plate.' I handed him the twenty bucks and the keys. 'They probably won't charge anything, but if they do . . .'

"He reached into his wallet and started taking something out. It was his driver's license.

"'What's this?' I said.

"'I don't want you to worry,' he said.

"'Forget it!' I said, handing it back. 'I'm not worried. I just need my car.'

"'Mustang, huh?' he said. Turns out he was a race-car mechanic.

"'All these Mustangs have the same problem,' he said, 'all the rubber in the front end dies after three years.'

"We talked for a while about cars. Then he went down and retrieved my car.

"I was just amazed at my good fortune. 'Where did you come from?' I said as he was getting ready to leave. 'Just hanging around in the lobby waiting for people to fall down so you can help them?'

"'No,' he said, 'my wife is upstairs with her mom, who is dying, and I came out to have a cigarette, and then I remembered I don't smoke anymore.'

"He was just a guy who fixes cars, his mother-in-law was

dying upstairs, and all he could think about was did I hurt my head, and did I need anything."

That was Phil's story.

We are always grateful when someone comes to our aid. If we fell flat on our face the way Phil did, in a hallway or on a sidewalk, we would hope that someone would come. Usually, someone does.

Occasionally, and sometimes tragically, no one comes. In 1964, the case of Kitty Genovese made headlines around the country. Ms. Genovese was stabbed to death one night on a Brooklyn street corner. Later, investigators discovered that more than thirty people heard or saw the attack from their apartment windows. But no one came to her aid. No one called the police. "I didn't want to get involved," they said.

This story, along with the phrase "I didn't want to get involved," became a cause célèbre in its day, a chilling example of how the traditional values of helping and caring had become lost in the jungle of urban life. In the nearly forty years since then, drive-by shootings, child kidnappings, and priest pedophilia have trumped it in shock value. But the moral question it raises still troubles us. When we pass the homeless person on the street and think, I'd like to help him, but I don't have time, we are tacitly acknowledging the inner pull of the Helper's Work, as well as the moment-to-moment struggle each of us goes through in deciding whether or not to act on it.

This struggle goes on all the time. Some people seem to have a special gift for helping. For others, it is the opposite.

KINDNESS IS SOCIETY

In his book *Cultivating Compassion*, Dr. Jeffrey Hopkins writes: "During a lecture while I was interpreting for the Dalai Lama, he said in what seemed to me to be broken English, 'Kindness is society.' That's a strange thing to say. At the time . . . I thought he meant kindness is important to society, kindness is vital to society. But he was saying that kindness is so important that we cannot have society without it. Society is impossible without it."

"Society is impossible without it." It is true that every society needs a great deal of kindness in it to function at all. But there are many kinds of societies, some kind, some cruel. Perhaps we should say, "A *workable* society is impossible without it." Not all people, not all societies, are workable. As much as we admire the courage of Father Kolbe, willingly sacrificing his life for a stranger, we also must remember that the story is not only about Kolbe and the stranger, it is about the commandant too. Kolbe's supreme compassion and the commandant's cruelty arise together, as two extremes of the human condition. In fact, society *is* possible without kindness, but it is the society of the tyrant, of the criminal and the sociopath. It is a society that no one wants, but sometimes is one people must endure. Indeed, for sociopaths, the Helper's Work looks like a sucker's game. They ask, "Why help anyone?"

Before we dismiss that question as the thinking of a diseased mind, we must remember that the sociopath's condition is the moral state of the infant. We begin life as dedicated narcissists. When we are babies, the needs of the self are supreme. Our first challenge is to bond with our mother and those immediately around us. Even after bonding and establishing a loving relationship with another, we do not become aware that others have needs as we do until around the age of two. This awareness continues to develop slowly and isn't complete until late adolescence. Even well into adulthood, some narcissistic patterns remain. The character struggle between helping ourselves and helping others continues throughout life.

Some do not complete this moral journey. Some don't even begin it—those unfortunate souls who suffer from "failure to bond." In the first challenge of life—to connect with the one who gave them life—they fail. As they grow older, they experience little anxiety, for anxiety occurs when we are afraid to lose what we love, and these people do not know love. They do, however, know anger, sensing that something vital is missing from their lives. Understanding such people can help us understand ourselves and our need to bond with at least one other person, someone whose welfare matters to us, for whom we are willing to sacrifice. That bond becomes the basis for the Helper's Work.

PROFESSIONAL HELPERS

One way to understand the qualities and dimensions of the Helper's Work is to look at those who do it for a living, those in the so-called helping professions—doctors, nurses, paramedics, social workers, policemen, firemen, and so on. These professional helpers often undergo many years of training, and they make it their business to help those who are in need, sometimes at the risk of their own lives. What each of us do occasionally, the helping professionals do day in and day out.

Why would someone want to do that?

I put the question to Christie, age fifty-five, a nurse for more than thirty years.

"I always wanted to be a nurse," she replied, "even as a little girl. I used to practice putting Band-Aids on my dolls."

"So for you this was a kind of calling, more than a career choice?"

"I suppose," she said. "I never really thought about it. I just find it very rewarding to help people when they are sick. It's so hard to be sick, and they need help so much."

"But it sounds as though you get a lot out of it too."

Christie beamed. "Of course!" she said. "It's what I love. I'd probably do it even if they didn't pay me."

"I'd probably do it even if they didn't pay me"—this is often the professional helpers' refrain, telling us that helping is not a one-way street, not a blood transfusion where we end up with less and the other more. The flow seems to go in both directions. Helping is mutual, even when it doesn't seem so.

A Zen student once asked Soen Roshi, a Japanese Zen master, "How can I encourage myself?"

His answer: "Encourage others."

Steve, the psychotherapist who told me this story, went on to say, "Soen Roshi was right. When I began my own therapy practice of helping others, I had a vivid experience of being tremendously helped myself. It was a significant motivation to continue on."

This mutuality is the secret of all compassionate activity. At the center of the process is this thing called self. Self is the central topic of spiritual study. As Dogen, the thirteenth-century Japanese Zen master, said, "To study Buddhism is to study the self." It is well known to all students of Buddhism that *anatman*—"no abiding self"—is a central tenet of Buddhist teaching. But when expressed that way—self as something to be denied—it has a negative feeling to it. Self, we think, has *some* reality, after all. Whose picture is on our driver's license? Who answers when someone calls our name?

"No self boundary" may be closer to the mark. After saying that "study of the self" is central, in the next sentence Dogen added, "To study the self is to forget the self." The so-called bubble of self really isn't a boundary. When seen clearly, it is a connection. And one of the easiest ways to experience this connection is to reach out through this bubble to another person. In that moment of reaching out, self doesn't disappear. It isn't diminished, it grows. The bubble opens to include more, and both the helper and the helped feel enhanced. As Christie, the nurse, said, "I just find it very rewarding to help people when they are sick."

Phil, whose profession was group-conflict resolution, had a different way of expressing this idea.

"Clearly," I said to him, "you have a gift for working with people, especially couples and groups in conflict. What is that gift? What is your secret?'

"I came to realize," he replied, "that nobody knows as much about being me as I do, and nobody knows as much about being you than you do. Once people start to appreciate that about one another, instead of being in conflict they start to care for each other, and help one another."

In other words, if I am in my bubble, and you are in yours, we are separate selves—alone, apart. Once our bubbles expand to include both of us, not only are we joined, we are both greater than we were before. "To study the self"—to look closely at who we really are in the world, at all our activities and relationships— "is to forget the self." This is how the Helper's Work helps us grow and become more awakened, more *buddha*. And in the process, we feel uplifted.

"Of course!" Christie said about her work as a nurse. "It's what I love. I'd probably do it even if they didn't pay me."

Beyond doctrine, beyond thoughts of self and no self, in helping we are joyful. Our emotional experience is one of pleasure.

CONCLUSION

Pleasure and pain: These two shape the contours of our abiding in the world. An apple is sweet, and good for us. The hemlock is bitter, and can kill us. The flower's fragrance enchants us; the stink of decay and disease repels us. From the pleasure we feel in helping others we know that it is a good thing. That feeling redeems the risks we may have taken, the sacrifices we may have endured. This is the paradox of compassion, and of the Helper's Work: The more we are willing to set aside the self, with its survival imperatives, the more the self is nourished.

We often think that compassion is the essence of helping, and as a motivating force, it is. The minute we feel what someone else feels—when we can say, as Phil did, "Nobody knows as much about being me as I do, and it's the same for you"—we want to help. But from the standpoint of effectiveness and longevity—the willingness to keep at it, for days, months, or years—compassion is not always sufficient. Buddhist teaching tells us that the inner life of helping progresses through stages, sometimes called the Four Illimitables. These four—friendliness, compassion, sympathetic joy, and equanimity—make up the spiritual curriculum that accompanies the Helper's Work. We need all four—and more—if we are not to falter and, like a flashing meteor, burn out as we fall.

Chapter 12

THE HELPER'S CONSCIOUSNESS: EQUANIMITY

❧

WE FEEL FOR OTHERS; that is why we help. So it would seem that the Helper's Consciousness ought to be compassion. And indeed, compassion is the starting point for helping. Without being able to feel another person's distress, without having that basic empathy, no genuine helping is possible. But instead of compassion we have made *Equanimity* the Helper's Consciousness. To understand why, we need to investigate the deeper layers of the Buddhist teaching about compassion. What we will find—and this is particularly important for professional helpers—is that there is a difference between compassionate feeling and compassionate activity, between wanting to help and being deeply and truly helpful. Equanimity is not some kind of transcendental distancing. This quality is not like ordinary calm, nor is it "detachment"—an English word often mis-understood in describing the attitude of a Buddha. Equanimity is being "all the way" for someone, being committed to their well-being within an attitude of steadiness, calm, and compo-sure. Real Equanimity is the compassion beyond compassion. Only with Equanimity can we really understand the Buddha's teaching about human suffering.

∽∞∽

We begin our investigation by taking up Buddhism's Four Illimitables—or, as Lama Surya Das calls them, the four Hearti-tudes—which are a Buddhist teaching for opening the heart of compassion. They are usually translated as friendliness, com-passion, sympathetic joy, and equanimity. Each of them includes a set of prayers and meditations. For example, the prayer for *metta,* or friendliness, is:

> May you be free from danger;
> May you be free from physical suffering;
> May you be free from mental suffering;
> May you have ease of well-being.

The object of these prayers changes as the meditation pro-gresses. First it is directed to ourselves: "May I be free from danger." Then it is to those we love and care about; gradually (and most difficult!) it may come to include even our enemies. Such a practice, when carried on for several days in the atmos-phere of a meditation retreat, can be very powerful. Doug reported this experience while on a meditation retreat: "On the fifth day, while walking and saying the mantra, I felt an explo-sion in my chest and experienced an incredible sense of loving every living creature. This was more profound than anything I had ever known before and lasted many hours."

Without the Heartitudes—each one of them—there is no chance of helping anyone. If our hearts are not open to others, their suffering goes unnoticed. It wouldn't even occur to us that they need our help. The cultivation of compassion is a central component of every spiritual tradition, and Buddhism has made an important contribution by providing us not just with teachings about compassion but spiritual exercises and meditations to build up the compassion circuits in our brains, to transform a prayer such as "May you have ease and well-being" from mere words to a transformative experience. Over time, compassion develops from something we feel into something we have become.

In his book *Buddhist Thought in India,* Dr. Edward Conze summarized the four Heartitudes as follows:

> Friendliness: May beings be happy!
> Compassion: How unhappy beings are!
> Sympathetic joy: Rejoice with these beings!
> Equanimity: Just beings!

Of the four Heartitudes, friendliness, or *metta,* is probably the most familiar to us, both because it is now widely taught in Buddhist centers such as the one Doug attended and because it meshes well with the familiar Christian teaching of brotherly love. Compassion, or *karuna,* is a natural extension of friendliness and is its deeper and more heartfelt cousin. Sympathetic joy, or *mudita,* is a concept for which there is no applicable word in English, though German has something close in the expression *freuden mit,* which is used colloquially to mean "I'm happy for you" but literally means "rejoice-with." Sympathetic joy is the pleasure we feel at someone else's good fortune. When the other person is our child, *mudita* is easy. When the other person is a fellow employee who just got promoted over us, we realize why *mudita* is considered a more advanced state than either friendliness or compassion.

∞

Equanimity, or *upekkha,* means a kind of transcendental even-mindedness in the face of any kind of suffering—the capacity to see "just beings," in Conze's words. This appears at first to imply some kind of distancing or detachment from the emotions of friendliness and compassion. How can this be the highest stage? All the emotion, the heartfelt feeling of friendliness and compassion, seems to have disappeared in equanimity. No more rejoicing, no more empathy, no more wishing for others' happiness. We are left only with a kind of impartiality, with "just beings." And yet this is said to be the most advanced Heartitude of all. Buddhist teaching tells us that this "divine impartiality" is far removed from the "dull indifference of foolish persons" and means cultivating a sense of universality in the way we view other people. With friendliness, compassion, and even sympathetic joy, there is always a tendency to apply these feelings just to *some* people—those we like, or those for whom we have sympathy, such as the poor or the oppressed. There is also a faint echo of "I" in the background— "I" who am feeling compassion. It is only in Equanimity that we are able to turn our compassion impartially to everyone and everything. Our natural feelings of empathy and compassion have developed to such a degree that we no longer discriminate in any way. Everyone becomes equally worthy of our concern.

These Heartitudes are essential for the Helper's Work. Because we feel another's difficulty, because we empathize with another's suffering, we naturally want to help. Our feeling leads us in that direction. But most helping can't become actualized unless we translate that feeling into some kind of helpful action or response. And feeling by itself does not guarantee that the actions we take are going to be helpful. We must also face the questions, What is really helpful? How do we know if we are really helping someone? We may think that all we need is the intention to help—that if our heart is in the right place, the correct response will come naturally. But in the complex realm of human relations this is not always so. In fact, sometimes good intentions can get in the way.

COMPASSION'S LIMITS

Amanda's sister, a drug addict, came to her pleading, "Just a hundred dollars. I'm broke. I'm behind on my rent. A hundred dollars, that's all I ask, and I promise, I'll never ask again. Starting tomorrow I'm going to get clean."

Amanda's heart breaks. She feels her sister's suffering so acutely. She wants to help her. She wants to believe that this time it will be different. Even though she knows or suspects that the hundred dollars will be spent on alcohol or drugs, even though she has been through this drama so many times before, Amanda reaches into her purse for the money, because she cannot bear to see her sister in such pain.

Did Amanda feel her sister's suffering? Of course she did. Was she compassionate and loving? Yes. Was her action helpful? Any professional substance abuse counselor knows the answer:

No. She was not really helping her sister, she was enabling her addiction. In fact, Amanda's well-meaning actions actually prolonged her sister's suffering. What the sister really needed was a dose of "tough love" to make her face her addiction and the suffering it was causing her and others. Often, close relatives or friends can't provide this kind of tough love; they are too emotionally involved. In such cases, professional help may be necessary.

∽∞∾

This example illustrates the limitations of empathy and compassionate feeling in being truly helpful. Amanda couldn't really be helpful to her sister, not because she wasn't compassionate but precisely because she *was* so compassionate. And even for professional helpers, if their underlying motivation begins and ends with compassion, they become susceptible to exhaustion and burnout. This is why the cultivation of Equanimity, in the Buddhist sense, is so important. In commonsense terms, it may seem as though Equanimity is the last of the Heartitudes to come on board: In fact, as Lama Surya Das says, in his Buddhist tradition Equanimity is taught not last but first, as the root of all true compassionate activity.

There are two reasons for this. First, at the mundane level, there is some limit to how far we can gradually expand our compassion, from those we love most to those we love least, before we burn out from the effort. Second, at the most transcendent level, we have to confront the existential question of "beings" themselves. Compassionate to whom? Is there really an "I" separate from others? Or is there a ground of Being that subsumes us all, out of which compassion naturally arises, not because it is something we have practiced but because it is something we all share, and that we all are? When we actually experience that we are not separate beings at all, but one great Being, the whole enterprise of compassionate activity is totally transformed. At the most transcendent level, this compassion of Equanimity need not always translate into a specific helpful action. This is how Buddhists understand the highest form of meditation and compassion—just sitting and being in the world, with Equanimity and impartiality, holding the suffering of every being and thing in our hearts.

This level of understanding is a tall order. In fact, it is quite difficult to comprehend intellectually. We need something more powerful and subtle than just thought or even feeling. We need the actual experience of sitting still, amid this Being, as well as a way to focus our intention and understanding. There is a name for this focus, a lens to concentrate our good intention, and that is *vow*.

EQUANIMITY AND VOW

What is a vow, really? How does it differ from an ordinary thought or a promise? What would happen if we substituted "vow" for "think"?

Suppose, instead of saying, "I'm thinking of going to the store to buy a candy bar," we say, "I *vow* to go." There is something a bit ridiculous about this statement. In real life no one would say, "I vow." We hardly need the horsepower of a word like *vow* to buy a candy bar. Our craving for sugar is motivation enough. Besides, eating a candy bar lasts only a few seconds, and then the craving is gone. The whole affair is too impulsive, too trivial, to justify a word like *vow*.

How about "I vow to punch him in the nose"? This, at least, is more serious. Our own nose might get bloodied; we might even end up in jail. But still, it is impulsive. No vow is necessary to motivate us; our anger is enough. If anything, we need a vow to restrain ourselves: "No matter how angry I am, I vow to act with dignity and restraint." A punch in the nose is more weighty than a candy bar, but hardly less impulsive.

"I vow to get back at him, even if it takes me the rest of my life." Now the word *vow* begins to fit the circumstance. This isn't an impulsive or momentary thought. Our revenge is one we intend to sustain for a long period of time. Of course, the thought in this case is a negative, angry one. In fact, this is one important difference between anger and hatred. Anger is a firecracker, bursting into flame and subsiding in a moment. Hatred is a fire that is constantly refueled, hundreds and thousands of times, by hateful thoughts.

"I vow to get back at him" is a real vow, of sorts, but a destructive one. In the end, it won't work. We know the saying "Revenge is a dish best served cold." What it doesn't say is that revenge is not food, it is poison. A destructive vow ends up destroying everything, including itself. It has power, and some longevity, but it doesn't last and doesn't work. For a vow to work, it has to be based not on deluded or hateful thinking but on reality, on the compassionate ground of Being itself.

❧

The first of the four Bodhisattva vow states, "However many beings there are in the world, I vow to liberate them all." This is not entirely unfamiliar. Exhortations to "love thy neighbor as thyself" can be found in every religious tradition. What distinguishes the Bodhisattva vow is its immense scope. Its commitment is not just to helping our neighbors or our community, but all people everywhere, as well as plants, animals, and the whole living world. Taken literally—"I vow to liberate *every* being"—it sounds absurd. How can we help every being in the world? And yet this vow is the core of Buddhist spiritual life. It includes the four Heartitudes and more. How can we take such a vow seriously without being overwhelmed by it?

That is why the Bodhisattva vow is so powerful and comprehensive. Given the number of beings we know there are in the world, it is obviously weighty. And Buddhism understands that its longevity transcends any one human life, and in its scriptures imagines Bodhisattvas toiling selflessly for the benefit of others for thousands, even millions of lifetimes. There is even a class of Buddhist folk tales—the Jataka tales—that are stories about the previous lifetimes of the Buddha, during which he prepared himself for his eventual spiritual destiny through lifetimes of selfless activity.

This vow is unattainable in any conventional sense of the word; it is literally inconceivable. A vow that can be perfectly attained retains, to the Buddhist sensibility, some subtle sense of self, a quality of ambition or accomplishment. For Buddhists, only a vow that cannot possibly be achieved qualifies as a vow worthy of the name.

EQUANIMITY IN ACTION

One day, in the early years of Tassajara monastery, Shunryu Suzuki lectured on this vow. At the end Suzuki said, "If sentient beings are numberless, our vow to save them seems very silly. But still we do it. Why? Because we don't feel so good if we don't work for others. Whether it is possible or not is not the question. Anyhow, do it! That is our vow."

Gordon, who was getting ready to be ordained as a Zen Buddhist priest, raised his hand and said, "When I promise to do something, it has to have some meaning. If it doesn't have some meaning I can't say it."

"That is because your effort is still based on some selfish idea," Suzuki replied.

Gordon started to cry.

In those days we were all beginners. Everything about Buddhism was new to us, and we relied on Suzuki-Roshi's kindness and patience to help us understand. After Gordon asked his question, I expected Suzuki-Roshi to respond in a gentle or comforting way, as he usually did.

Suzuki and Gordon discussed this point for some time, each of them trying to explain to the other what he meant. In the end, Suzuki said, "Maybe if I were your age I could agree with you quite easily and we would be great friends, but now I am not your friend."

Gordon remained sitting on his cushion, continuing to weep, but Suzuki said nothing more, sitting impassive and unsmiling—sitting, we might say, in Equanimity—until, after what seemed a long while, someone else raised his hand and asked another question.

A few days later Gordon withdrew as a candidate for ordination.

During the Buddha's lifetime, the term for "teacher" was *kalyanamitra,* or "good spiritual friend." That was the role of a senior monk or nun in the life of a junior one, the role of an elder brother or sister, a mentor or guide. In those early years of Tassajara, Suzuki-Roshi was indeed a good spiritual friend to all of us. He laughed with us, took baths with us, worked and ate with us—and early in the morning or late at night, he was always there doing *zazen* in the meditation hall with us.

And yet to Gordon he said, "I am not your friend."

It was a shock to hear him say that. Why wouldn't he be

Gordon's friend? I knew how sincere Gordon was, how heart-felt was his desire to practice Buddha's way fully and completely. I didn't understand Suzuki's attitude. His equanimity seemed like harshness to me. Was he trying to be Gordon's friend in some deeper way? Was this a Buddhist form of "tough love"?

EQUANIMITY AND BURNOUT

There are six billion humans, not to mention innumerable other creatures. Does the vow include plant life too? The original language is clear: It says "all beings." Tomato plants and dahlias are certainly beings; they have life just as we do. Plants, animals, insects, jellyfish—the vow includes all of them. Members of all the insect species alone, biologists tells us, run into the trillions. If we try to count the number of beings one by one, it seems hopeless. We will, like Gordon, be discouraged.

When we see one person suffering, or a hundred, we are moved to tears. But what about a thousand? A million? A billion? Our reservoir of good feeling has its limits. We can take only so much and then we succumb. We are exhausted, we burn out. This can happen with people in the helping professions—doctors, nurses, therapists. When the "ratio strain" gets too great—when too much of our compassion is flowing out and not enough nourishment is coming back—we falter.

I once sat in a meeting with Kristen, a well-known environmental activist. As the meeting droned on about procedural matters and budgets, she said nothing. But finally, when there was a pause in the conversation, she exploded. "This meeting is like torture for me!" she exclaimed. "What does it matter? This is a waste of time. I need to be out doing the work." She never came to the meeting again.

At first I was impressed with her commitment, her zeal for "the work." Her compassion for the depredations of our planet was deep and sincere. But as I thought further, there was something about her outburst that made me uncomfortable. While we sat in the living room and talked, no seals were being saved, no oil spills cleaned, no polluted streams purified. So, was her impatience really helping? Could she really be effective in such a state of mind?

Her commitment and compassion were obvious and sincere, but something was missing, some broad perspective, some ability to hold all of her zeal in some larger embrace. What was missing was Equanimity. When professional helpers are on the edge of burnout, compassion can begin to turn into irritability, exhaustion, or even pain. Or as Sam, once a relief worker in the refugee camps in Nicaragua, put it, "I think in those days my wanting to help was a kind of martyrdom I used to escape my own pain." As long as we imagine that the Helper's Work is like climbing a mountain, a set of finite tasks, a mission to be accomplished, at some point we might falter and wonder how we can go on.

EQUANIMITY AND THE IMPOSSIBLE VOW

So, what is the way out? How can we accomplish the vow? Perhaps we can find a clue in a passage from Suzuki's book *Zen Mind, Beginner's Mind:*

"Suppose your children are suffering from a hopeless disease. You do not know what to do; you cannot lie in bed. Normally the most comfortable place for you would be in a warm comfortable bed, but now because of your mental agony you cannot rest. You may walk up and down, in and out, but this does not help. Actually the best way to relieve your mental suffering is to sit *zazen,* even in such a confused state of mind and bad posture. If you have no experience of sitting in this kind of difficult situation you are not a Zen student."

When our child is dying, we want to help. We would do anything to help. But we can't. There is nothing we can do. We don't have time to go on retreat and try to cultivate more friendliness, love, and compassion. Anyway, we already have these feelings for our child in abundance. This is our child, after all! We love her more than anything. We would do anything for her. But we are helpless. What can we do? Walking back and forth won't help, Suzuki says. Going to bed won't help. Sleeping pills and tranquilizers won't help. What can we do? Just sit, he says. Sit.

This is pretty tough teaching. Why, exactly, does he recommend this? To calm ourselves down? To make ourselves feel just a little better? That is not quite right. Nothing will make us feel better. Anyway, it's not that we want to feel better, we want our *child* to feel better. And she won't, not ever again. We feel lost. Equanimity in any ordinary sense is impossible.

To really help another person, we have to be all the way for them. If we are anxious, panicked, conflicted, heartbroken—all of which we would feel at the bedside of our dying child— some part of ourselves is not available, something is being held back. When we are fully there, fully alert, unencumbered by our own feelings, our own "stuff"—only then can we be helpful in the deepest sense.

It stung me to hear Suzuki say to my friend Gordon, "Your effort is still based on your selfish practice." Gordon wasn't a selfish person, and he didn't seem to be acting selfishly while asking his question about the Bodhisattva vow. Much later, I came to realize that Suzuki was not talking about ordinary self-ishness. He was talking about unconditional and unlimited selflessness, the kind we need at the bedside of our dying child, or in the face of our struggling planet, or in the full awareness that myriads of people and beings are suffering and dying—most needlessly—every day. It seems to be an impossibly high standard. And it is. It is precisely *because* it is impossible that we can do it, that we have to do it.

And yet if we are too grim about it, if we take the whole matter too seriously, that is not quite right either. Gordon's tears were genuine enough, but how can we help even one being—even ourselves—when we are crying in frustration, when we take the task so seriously? In transcendental compassion, we have to walk like an elephant—not too slowly, not too fast, not too emotionally involved, not too emotionally detached, maintaining a calm and indefatigable demeanor.

This is the equanimity that knows no bounds, and yet has room for the inconceivable fulfillment of an impossible vow.

THE HELPER'S WORK AND THE CONSCIOUSNESS PROJECT

The Consciousness Project is only a little bit about our own inner work and mostly about how we share that work with others. This point is well made in accounts of the life of Gautama the Buddha. Just after his enlightenment, the Buddha at first thought that no one would understand what had happened to him under the Bodhi tree. "It will be difficult for mankind to understand," he said to himself.

But the king of the gods entreated him to reconsider. "Let the Perfect One teach the Dharma!" he said. "For there are beings in the world whose sight is but little clouded."

That was the moment that the Buddha came down the mountain and rejoined society as a religious teacher.

However great or small our spiritual understanding, our task is to look to the right and to the left, and see whom we can join, and with whom we can share what we know.

QUESTIONS TO ASK, THINGS TO DO

On another occasion, Suzuki said, "To liberate one being is to liberate all beings." Again, using the ordinary calculus of the rational mind, this may seem a cop-out. Kristen, the environmental activist, would probably say, "One is not enough! The planet is dying!"

But again, Suzuki was speaking not from his rational mind but from the standpoint of Equanimity, which rests in the confidence that when we fully address the needs and circumstances of one being, we address the greater Being that all of us share.

Can you think of one person, one being for whom you can be all the way? Your partner, perhaps, or your child? Your superior or subordinate at work? Are you willing to try adopting an attitude of calmness and Equanimity toward that person and, in a sense, vow to stay with the relationship, whatever the person's needs and your capacity to address them, to the end?

If you really can do it all the way, then one person *is* enough. And also not enough. Let it be one person at time, stepping slowly and carefully through the time and space that is your life, the way an elephant progresses through the forest, helping where you can, letting be where you cannot.

The practice of Equanimity is not really something to be understood but rather something to be embraced.

Chapter 13

THE PARENT'S WORK

❧

I ASKED FRANK, "Why are you a plumber?" and his immediate answer was, "To make a living." But when we ask someone, "Why are you a parent?" the answer is not so obvious. Some would simply say, "I love children." Others wouldn't see the point of the question. They would simply answer, "Isn't that what life is all about?"

At one level, reproduction is indeed what life is all about— the biological imperative of all species. In that sense, there is no reason, no "why." In fact, if nature had left human reproduction up to reason, we might have died out long ago. In evolutionary terms, judgment and reason are recent additions to our psychic arsenal. The urge to reproduce, to bring a new generation into the world, is more ancient and powerful than any thought.

Until recently, parenting was also closely tied to physical survival. Having children was a way of producing more hands to till the fields, tend the livestock, cobble the shoes. In traditional societies, infant mortality was high. People had many children simply to ensure that a few would live.

Reproduction is also more labor-intensive for us than any other species. A male salmon need do no more than spray his seed into the water to accomplish his reproductive mission. The mother crocodile stands guard over her babies only until they have grown large enough to find food and defend themselves. The mother bear teaches her cubs the skills of hunting and the means of survival for two years, but after that she abandons them. Human children are the most helpless of all. Without adults to care for them, they would not survive at all. We are all born with an enormous need to be cared for. We are also born with an equally compelling desire and need to love and care for our children. A good thing, too. The work of being a human parent—eighteen years of in-house nurturing, and then a lifetime of concern and care from a distance—is enormous.

Nevertheless, most people take on this heroic job willingly and lovingly. Larry and his wife did. In addition to raising his six children, he and his wife regularly volunteered to take in troubled children from other families. When I asked Larry why they did that, he explained that it was a matter of how he himself was raised:

"When I was growing up we always had friends stay over at the house and my Dad loved that. We really liked the expanded family. In our family the best thing you could do was help somebody else. It didn't have to be with money. We used to joke about being so poor we couldn't pay attention let alone the rent.

"I was corn-fed and hand-spanked in about fifteen different languages because the people in our neighborhood—the parents of the children I went to school with—were immigrants from Greece, Romania, Russia, Germany, Mexico, Italy, China. We knew people from all those places at the same time."

It sounded to me as though Larry's whole neighborhood was an extended family for him. No wonder he was so comfortable adding other people's children to his biological family. His story also reminds us how much our parenting styles are modeled after our own parents—for good or ill—and how deeply embedded is the desire to nurture children and the joy we find in it.

"Altogether, how many kids other than your own did you take in?" I asked Larry.

"Eleven altogether. Not all at once, of course. We wound up going to three of the girls' weddings. When you do something like that there's the satisfaction that you really put somebody's feet on a straight path, teaching them how to be open and honest and trustworthy. It was just fabulous."

Larry saw being a surrogate parent not as hard work (though it surely must have been) but as something "fabulous," something that brought him deep satisfaction. His experience reminds us that though parenting is a lot of work, it is also the source of our deepest joy. On the outside, what appears to be work can feel, on the inside, like the most wonderful and satisfying thing we do as human beings.

Parents rarely weigh the cost versus the benefit before plunging in. Most parents are willing to sacrifice anything—money, time, even, in extreme circumstances, their own lives—to care for and protect their children. Compare this dedication to that of even the most loyal corporate employee and we see that being a parent is work of another order entirely. Parenting is, more than any paying job, the Great Work. When people look back and reflect on their lives, it is generally their work as parents—not their salesperson-of-the-year awards—that makes them most proud.

CHALLENGES OF THE PARENT'S WORK

We might think that for such important work, the one that gives our lives so much satisfaction and meaning, we would take care to provide the best training, better than for any occupation or livelihood. But parents typically do not receive any formal training. We have always learned how to parent from our own parents. In addition to them, there used to be aunts and uncles or other adults in the community to help. *It Takes a Village to Raise a Child,* the title of Senator Hillary Clinton's bestselling book, says it all. But in our society that village—both as a physical and a metaphorical place—is fast vanishing. Soon it will be gone, replaced by families living in isolation from one another. Larry's melting-pot neighborhood is no longer common. For today's families, neighbors are not friends but strangers—or, as we read in the newspaper to our horror, in rare occasions even molesters or abductors. Grandparents may live a continent away. Aunts and uncles are a presence only on holidays. These days parenting is more lonely than it once was. Often it is just two (and sometimes not even two) inexperienced people struggling to find out *how* to parent in the middle of parenting. And unless their child's behavior is egregious, no one intervenes. No one helps. And even when they do, that help is a poor substitute for the real thing.

When Sharon was searching for a child to adopt, she met Jenny at a children's shelter. Children were supposed to be there only six weeks, but Jenny had been there for months. She had already been in and out of six foster homes. Sharon wanted to adopt a child because she wanted to share her good fortune. She also wanted to find a child for whom she could make a difference, one who was "helpable." Jenny certainly needed her help. After Sharon adopted Jenny, she discovered that Jenny kept with her a collection of "treasures"—one of which was the crumpled business card of a sheriff's deputy. "Call this number and someone will help you" the deputy had told her after one of many visits to the home of Jenny's biological family, where she had been regularly abused. Jenny had kept that card with her for years.

It has been said, "Judge the health of a society by how it takes care of its sick, its old, and its children." If this is the standard by which we measure ourselves, then Jenny's story—an all-too-common one—is indeed an indictment. When I asked Sharon what it was like taking on a child like Jenny, with her history of abuse, she replied, "It almost defeated me the first two years. It was so hard, having to confront the evil side of the human community in a direct, personal way. Most people never have to do that."

The Dalai Lama has expressed puzzlement about Western-ers' difficult family histories and lack of self-esteem, factors that make it harder for us to cultivate Buddhist friendliness and compassion, especially for ourselves. Stories such as Jenny's are one reason. Of course, those of us with these problems are not spiritually deficient, just deficiently parented. Another lesson is that parents, for good or ill, help lay the foundation for adult spiritual life; in other words, for better or worse, our parents are our first spiritual teachers.

Sharon had wanted to adopt a child because, she said, "I felt that I had more than enough in my life. I wanted to give some-thing back." These days parents come in many flavors: adoptive parents like Sharon, gay parents, foster parents, volunteer par-ents like Larry, even institutional parents. The desire to have biological offspring is deep and real; but the desire to parent a child, any child, seems equally deep and real. Otherwise, how do we explain the fervor with which childless couples seek to adopt, or the enthusiasm of gay parents to be accorded the same rights as heterosexual ones in the eyes of society and the law?

These issues seem more problematic for adults than for the children themselves. Children are remarkably resilient in recognizing as a parent any caring adult who seems willing and able to be one. We may make too much of biological parenthood. Jenny's real parents were a disaster for her. How fortunate for her that she and Sharon found each other!

The Parent's Work in this wider sense includes a variety of roles that adults perform with children: family, teacher, camp counselor, coach, den mother, and so on. In an urban society of near-strangers this role of extended parent has limits, though. Try mediating between a shouting parent and a bawling child in any public place—a role that would probably be welcomed in most traditional village cultures—and we quickly discover that this readiness to take communal responsibility for children has deteriorated in ours. The Parent's Work, at one time the responsibility of all adults, has, like so much else in our modern world become segmented and institutionalized. The village and small-town network of trusted friends and neighbors has largely been replaced by a diverse society of strangers.

THE PARENT'S WORK AS SPIRITUAL WORK

The Parent's Work is more than just the exterior task of raising children. It has a spiritual dimension too. Being a parent is an unparalleled opportunity to develop the traditional spiritual virtues of love and generosity, as well as to be our children's first and most intimate spiritual mentor, teaching them by example and by instruction the basics of an ethical and compassionate life. One would think that parents ought to be lauded and showcased in every spiritual tradition as true spiritual heroes. The reality is that until recently there has often been a tendency to see the Parent's Work as incompatible with a serious spiritual life. The Hindu *sadhu,* or world-renouncing ascetic, abjured sexuality as a distraction and a drain on the psychic energy needed for spiritual liberation. The priests of some cults in ancient Greece castrated themselves as a sacrifice to their god. The founder of Christianity never married, and to this day Catholic monks, nuns, and priests take vows of lifelong celibacy. The founder of Buddhism abandoned his family, and for most of its history Buddhism also required lifelong celibacy of its monks and nuns.

Over the last century things have changed. These days there are movements afoot in all these traditions to reexamine this alienation between family life and spirituality. Catholics are questioning the value and psychological effect of priestly celibacy, while many of the best priests leave the priesthood to marry and raise families. Most Western Buddhist teachers have families and children and are doing their best to integrate the demands of traditional Buddhist spiritual life—such as meditation retreats—with job and family.

All this is most welcome. The recognition that the Parent's Work can itself be a spiritual path is long overdue, and is consistent with the wider reexamination of old beliefs that is going on throughout our society. We now understand much more clearly how important it is to begin life in the care of adults who love us and treat us with kindness and respect, and we understand how many of society's ills can be traced to poor parenting. To love and be loved—is this not the essence of all spiritual traditions? What better time to learn this than at the beginning of life, and what better time to practice these virtues than when we are parents ourselves!

As for Buddhism, its fresh challenge in the West is to see the family not as a distraction from the spiritual path but as an integral part of it. This is not inconsistent with the life of traditional Buddhist societies. Anyone who has spent time in a Buddhist country such as Thailand or Vietnam knows that traditional family life there is full of warmth and love. Buddhist temples often abound with youngsters playing their games while their parents worship within, and Buddhist priests genuinely enjoy the company of these children. In these Asian countries, the Buddhist values of patience and compassion are well integrated into family life.

And why should it be otherwise? Is not the ability to sustain a marriage or other intimate relationship over a long period an important test of personal and spiritual maturity? Is not the challenge of sustaining an intimate, loving relationship with another person as important as the quest for enlightenment— in fact, a part of that quest?

There are no "parent sutras" in Buddhism's core literature, no spiritual heroes whose great accomplishment was that they remained committed to a long-term relationship and raised a happy, loving family. If we consider the Bodhisattva vow to care for and save all beings as the linchpin of the Buddhist worldview, then this lack of parent sutras seems odd. What better practice for a Bodhisattva-in-training than caring for one's own children? In this sense, the Bodhisattva vow is an extension of the love and compassion we feel for our own children—the Bodhisattva as transcendental parent! If we can find no parent sutras in the Buddhist literature, then it becomes our responsibility to write them.

Having said all this, there is still a place in our modern world for the traditional, celibate monastic, and there are many who are following that path with vigor and sincerity. They too can do the Parent's Work—not necessarily by raising children but by operating in society as a parent would. This is the ideal of the Catholic priest too, the "father" who abjures private family in favor of his parishioners, his larger spiritual family. We have seen, though, in the recent scandals in the Catholic Church, how difficult it is to tread this path with maturity and grace. There is a tendency for a vow of celibacy to have the effect not of eliminating sexuality but of driving it underground in unhealthy ways. We live in an age of honesty and full disclosure. That kind of "as if" behavior—a professed celibate who really isn't—is no longer acceptable, if it ever was.

PARENT AS PROTECTOR

When we are children, we want our parents to love us and care for us; that is their primary role. But parents have another role, just as important: They help us feel safe. All children are acutely aware of how vulnerable they are, how much they need someone older and stronger to look out for their well-being. These days children are asking (and parents must try somehow to reassure them) about anthrax, about terrorists and airplanes being flown into tall buildings. Childhood is fraught with enough real or imagined fear without these indications of a world gone mad, but it is the world in which we now live. In addition to their own fears and anxieties about these new terrors, adults need to find some way to satisfy their children's need to preserve the illusion that they are safe.

As adults, we know that the world is full of dangers. No one is really safe. But our children need the *illusion* of safety. They need Dad to tell them stories to chase away their bad dreams. They need Mom to hug them when they fall and cut their knees. When children climb into bed to go to sleep, they need to feel that Mom and Dad (or Dad and Dad, or whoever their functioning parents may be) will watch over them and protect them from harm. Nothing can be more damaging to a growing child, or to the adult the child will one day become, than to be robbed of this sense of security. If we have it as children, we can grow into strong, courageous adults who can face the real risks and dangers of life—including the risks of an intimate relationship—without recoiling or shrinking back.

But even adults need to be protected. We saw after September 11 how much admiration and respect welled up for the police and firefighters who sacrificed their lives to save people in the burning buildings. Even soldiers—when their jobs are defensive and not predatory—can perform this role for us.

Richard said that this was why he became a policeman, to serve this role. To illustrate, he told me this story:

"We got a call that there was a woman in an apartment unconscious. Maybe it was a heart attack, maybe a drug overdose, we didn't know. The paramedics were on their way, but my partner and I were closer. As soon as we got there and saw her lying there—she couldn't have been more than nineteen—we knew she was gone. We went through the motions, but we knew. Her father was there, sitting in a chair, crying, hoping against hope. It was our job to break the news as gently as we could. And then there's that awkward time when we just stand around, witnesses to the death scene, waiting for the paramedics to come, trying to think of something to say or do to comfort the father, knowing there was nothing, really. You realize then that just being there as a cop, playing that role at the worst moment in a person's life, is what the job is all about."

We tend to stereotype cops as tough men and women who arrest the bad guys, but as Richard explained, the case of the dead girl and her father is more the norm. "Being there at the worst moment in a person's life"—that is what we count on our parents to do for us, and that is what Richard and his partner did for the girl's father.

In the same way as parents provide a safety net for their children, these defenders do so for the whole society. In a certain sense, they too are performing the Parent's Work. In times of peace and prosperity, their work is less visible and therefore less appreciated. But in the same way as children know that they are not strong enough to protect themselves, and count on their parents to do it for them, average citizens look to their professionally trained protectors.

This is the Parent's Work as protector, and we must respect those who are willing to play that role in our lives, even at the risk of their own.

PARENTING AS GIVING

What unites all these different parental roles is a quality not only of giving but of *unconditional* giving. In ordinary giving, such as mailing a donation to the United Way, there is a sense of deliberation and choice, not to mention some reciprocal benefit—a tax deduction. But the parent does not think: Shall I feed my child today? Shall I send him to school, or am I too tired to bother? When the child runs ahead into the street, the parent does not think: I wonder if saving my child is worth the risk? No, she rushes into oncoming traffic and scoops her child up with little thought for her own safety. The calculating mind is little involved when it comes to the welfare of our children. We act unconditionally, and if anyone asked us why, we would reply: Because he is my child!

This holds true even for the professionals of public safety, who expect, and are expected, to risk their lives for the sake of

others. "To die for one's country" seemed an outmoded sentiment in the 80s and 90s, but that may be only because memories are short, and until recently there had not been much
pressing need for anyone to do so. There is no more unconditional act than offering what is most precious to us—our own
lives—for the benefit of others. The touchstone of the Parent's
Work is not just ordinary helping but a sense of readiness to sacrifice our own well-being, even our own survival, for the benefit of our children, or those we have sworn to protect as though
they were our children.

It is this "transcendent giving" that is the subject of the
next chapter.

Chapter 14

THE PARENT'S CONSCIOUSNESS: GIVING

THE WORD *GIVE,* like *work,* lies at the lowest stratum of language, describing something quite basic. There are many kinds of giving, but at its most elemental, giving is about material things. I have some food. I could eat it, but I do not. Instead, I hold it out to you. You accept it. That is my gift to you. This kind of giving is part of life's ordinary interchange and is usually conditional, related to some expectation of return. I expect something for my gift—if not a material thing, then something immaterial—your friendship, trust, and support. I give, but I also hope to get.

This is particularly true when we are young. As children of four or five, we understand giving primarily in terms of our own gratification. We give to get, we trade objects or favors with our immediate self-interests uppermost. "Remember what I said about sharing!" is the refrain of the parent struggling to remind two children playing with one set of toys. As our sense of self expands, we learn that generosity is part of being mature. We also form intimate bonds with others, fall in love, marry, and experience firsthand the feeling that giving is its own reward; the pleasure of others in receiving our gifts becomes our own pleasure.

This generosity of the mature adult is the starting point for the Buddhist practice of *dana,* which means giving, or generosity; in its most mundane sense, it refers to the donations that laypeople give to their Buddhist temple or center. "Please be generous with your *dana,*" a Buddhist leader might say at the conclusion of a meditation session or retreat. But as a spiritual practice, *dana* refers to the transformation of self and consciousness that leads to selfless giving, unconditional giving.

We have already explored one aspect of this practice in the Heartitudes—friendliness, compassion, sympathetic joy, and equanimity, which develop a spirit of generosity and care. At the root of these practices, however, and of the practice of *dana,* is the central issue of the self. The question of self underlies all acts of giving. "I give to you" is composed of three elements: I, you, and the gift. Of these, understanding the "I" is most important, because in the end the quality of the gift, its essence, lies not in what it is or in how you receive it, but in the consciousness and intention of the giver, the "I." When the "I" is capable of giving without any thought of return, Buddhism calls this not just *dana* but *dana paramita,* the "perfection" of giving. The perfect gift, the unconditional gift, transcends the boundaries of "I give and you receive." In the perfect gift, all narrow sense of self recedes, all sense of separation between giver and receiver melts away.

UNCONDITIONAL GIVING

If we consider the Heartitudes as practices to slowly, gradually loosen the boundaries of ordinary self, then it would seem that the ability to give unconditionally is a far-off spiritual goal, one that requires long effort and patience to strengthen our generosity muscles. But when we see that underlying the Heartitude practices, indeed all Buddhist practices, is the central issue of self, then the notion of unconditional giving takes on a different color. For whenever the bonds of self are loosened, whenever we set aside fear and self-protection, generosity and the spirit of selfless giving are not some far-off spiritual goal. They are immediately present.

How does this immediacy of selfless giving happen? This question harks back to the age-old question about the essential nature of a human being. If we think of ourselves as innately flawed, predisposed to selfish, destructive behavior, and scarred with original sin, then our effort to be generous, giving, loving beings becomes a constant struggle against our lower nature. If, on the other hand, we see our essential nature as fundamentally pure, just obscured and hidden from view by our misunderstanding of the nature of the self, then our effort becomes not a struggle with our nature but a struggle with the perceptions and attitudes that cloud it. Anyone familiar with the Buddhist worldview will immediately recognize that it espouses the latter view. It is not so much that we must learn to be generous and loving, says the Buddhist, but simply that we must see through that which prevents us from being generous and loving.

Both views of human nature can point to the evidence of history and personal experience to support their positions. The injustice and cruelty that human beings have imposed on one another from time immemorial is used to support the first view. How can we be innately good if we behave so badly? But we also know that in a crisis, our innate loving nature can burst out of its cocoon of defensiveness and fear. The aftermath of the terrorist attacks of September 11 is one example, when the whole country was suddenly united in an outpouring of generosity and appreciation for the fragility and preciousness of our collective lives. For the moment, self-centered attitudes were set aside.

An even more common example is one we explored in the preceding chapter—parenthood. The Parent's Work can evoke a quality of care and unconditional love for our child that can be overwhelming in its power. Who is this tiny, mewling being, warm and squirmy in our arms, who calls up such deep feelings of protectiveness and love, so that even the most macho or taciturn father is reduced to silly smiles and cooing? Whenever the love for a child is so all-encompassing and complete that considerations of self-benefit vanish, there is no asking why. As parents, we just give—unconditionally.

Even when the child is not biologically ours, the feelings are much the same. In chapter 13 we saw how Sharon's interest in adopting Jenny was closely connected to a sense of wanting to give. As she said, "I was looking for a situation where I could offer unconditional emotional acceptance." The inner work of parenting is to abide in this "unconditional emotional acceptance." For this helpless being who depends on us for everything, we are willing to do anything. The Parent's Work is one of many ways we can all take a first step down a path beyond the worldly and into the spiritual path.

Of course, this ideal of parenthood does not always comes to pass. There are parents such as Jenny's who reject their children, who are still children themselves and see their offspring only as whining burdens. The hurt and damaged children cast off in these situations are a testament to this failure. Even among ordinary parents, our relations to our children are often clouded by the same obscurations that afflict all human relations—pride, anger, selfishness, and greed. But most parents know that it is not uncommon for the clouds to part and our unconditional generous nature to shine through. Any loving parent who has nursed a child through a serious illness knows this to be true.

And as long as the Parent's Work extends only to our own children, or to our extended family's or clan's or tribe's children, it can still coexist with much darker feelings toward others whom we see as not like us, not of our color, language, culture, or religion. It is only when we are willing to extend that parental quality of unconditional giving not just to those near and dear to us but to everyone that we begin to approach the level of generosity taught by Buddha, and indeed by all great spiritual teachers.

The love of parent for child serves as a model, an entry point, the place where the biological imperative of caring for offspring intersects with the spiritual opportunity to become more than ourselves, to be awakened, to understand that each of us is a part of a larger whole in which we all have a responsibility and to which we all must contribute.

This is the parental as well as the spiritual ideal, and we all know that in reality most of us fall short of it much of the time. What is important about the ideal is not whether we achieve it but that it can be a conduit into a deeper issue of who we are in the world. To ask "Who am I?" in isolation from others is a monkish, reclusive endeavor. But to ask it in the context of an intimate relationship with another person—which is itself an important part of unconditional giving—is richer and deeper.

This can be the model of unconditional giving in the wider world, even to those whom we find difficult to love.

SELF AND SELFLESSNESS

What is important about the self is not so much whether it really exists but that each of us behaves as though it does. When someone asks Elizabeth at a party, "Who are you?" he is not looking for a metaphysical treatise. Elizabeth simply replies, "I am Elizabeth." But she is doing more than giving her name; "Elizabeth" is the label for that indelible sense of "me" that she carries with her from morning to night, that thing with a history, a will, with thoughts and feelings and—most of all—a keen interest in continuing.

But in the spiritual realm, the question "Who am I?" does not ask for labels or convenient names. We are looking beyond "that thing with a history." What we want to know, beneath all that, is the innermost quality of self. What is its nature? Shunryu Suzuki, with his preference for plain language, called it simply "big mind." As a concept, big mind is vague, difficult to grasp. It is not "me," yet it is not wholly other than "me," either. As an abstraction, it seems opaque. But when we see big mind at work in the world, when we observe its quality of compassion and care, it becomes clearer. Big mind is the mind that gives freely, that knows no limit. The person acting from the standpoint of big mind knows how to give without holding anything back.

If big mind is our essential nature, and if we can see it springing to life in crisis, in parenthood, or in a loving, intimate relationship to another, then why do we not have access to it all the time? Why—to echo the darker view of human nature—do people act with such cruelty and injustice to one another? And in the context of the Parent's Work, why can we not be kind, loving parents all the time? What is holding us back?

One answer is fear, the kind connected with survival, and the deeply imprinted neural circuits that we all possess, to fight or run to protect our very existence. And human beings alone among all creatures are conscious of that indelible sense of "me." The sense of "me," the highest level of organization of the psyche, exacts a price from the organism, and that price is a boundary, a barrier that separates it from what it is not. And around that barrier is a circle of fear. Fear holds up "me," keeps it afloat in the ocean of nonbeing, like a flotation device. Fear is the silent partner in our corporation of one—usually invisible but always watchful. Whenever we lapse from our stance as loving parent, whenever we feel that we are too exhausted or frustrated to give and keep giving, that is the flotation collar of fear at work, making big mind recede and small-mindedness loom.

Dr. Seymour Boorstein has noted that often a dying person experiences, and expresses, a feeling of unconditional warmth and love. He goes on to say that the reason for this sudden transformation at the point of death is the realization that "Death is happening *right now!*" In other words, the mission of our fear, its job of protecting the territory of self, has suddenly become unnecessary. And at that point, our innate loving nature can shine through. The same thing can happen when our child is in danger—when the little one we love so much is threatened. For a moment we have that same realization: Nothing matters! Move, jump, run! Protect the child. Being a parent is one of the ways we can become conscious of the constricting collar of self, and experience, at least in a crisis, how it can suddenly disappear. The Parent's Work is one of the most universal ways to experience the realm of big mind, at least for a moment.

MOMENTS OF LIFE-GIVING

This realization occurs not just in parenting. In fact, life itself is always bringing us these moments, as the following story illustrates.

Paul had just moved into a spiritual center in the heart of a large city. The neighborhood had recently been plagued by daytime burglaries. Several times a tan Chevrolet had been seen leaving the scene, but no one had been able to get a close look. The police seemed not to be aggressively pursuing the case. Chaz, a friend of Paul's who had lived in the city for years, and knew that Paul was an amateur photographer, had this suggestion: "Next time someone spots the Chevrolet, take a picture of it. That'll get the police off their duffs."

One day someone reported to Paul that the Chevrolet was parked at a nearby street corner. Paul grabbed his camera, with its telephoto lens, and headed out the door. As he approached the corner, he realized that the car was occupied, its four occupants just emerging. Holding the camera belt-high, and trying to be unobtrusive, Paul quickly snapped their picture. But just at that moment the head of the group happened to look Paul's way.

"Hey!" he shouted, and all four men began running toward him.

Frightened, Paul ran. The four men caught up to him at the front gate of his apartment building.

"Nobody takes my picture!" the ringleader said. "Give me that film!"

Paul didn't know what to do. His mouth was dry. His heart raced. The four men crowded around him. He glanced up and down the street but saw no one nearby.

"Who the hell you think you are?" the man shouted at him, jabbing a finger in Paul's face.

Something in the question jogged Paul out of his immobility and fear. He stuck out his hand. "I'm Paul," he said. "How you doing?"

Without thinking, the ringleader took Paul's outstretched hand. But only for a moment. Then he snatched his hand away with an expression of disgust.

"Okay," Paul said. "You want the film, take it." He opened the camera, took out the film, and handed it to the man.

The ringleader unspooled the film and held it up to the sun. "Damn right," he said. He stuffed the film into his jacket pocket and squinted at Paul, trying to figure him out. "I see you around, I'll kick your ass," he said finally.

Then he and his companions stalked away.

Later, Paul told this story to Chaz. "I was just trying to get a picture of the car," he said.

"The *empty* car, the *empty* car," Chaz said, shaking his head. "Man, you were lucky."

"Yeah," Paul said. "Lucky."

⬦

The fear that impedes us becomes, in the end, our guide. Whenever fear leaps into our throat, we know that we have touched the third rail that surrounds us, and can sense the direction in which we need to go. At the same time, the fear of unconditional giving points us toward unconditional giving. Much of the value of our gift to the one who receives it lies in the effort we made to reach past our selfish needs. The recipient of our gift is grateful because we had a choice, and chose to give. It could have gone the other way, as it so often does. We often treat one another with mutual suspicion and unease. We are so guarded that any break in the fence, any moment of connection, is a joy.

Our children know this instinctively. In spite of our mistakes as parents, our doubts and exhaustion, our selfishness and inattention, our children live for those moments when the clouds part and we can love them all the way. This is the nourishment that lets them grow. Thankfully, they are forgiving. They don't expect or need us to be perfect, only to do our best.

Both the unconditional gift and the mind that knows no bounds occur through, around, and because of the barrier of fear.

Fear can be our guide.

GIVING AND THE
CONSCIOUSNESS PROJECT

From the beginning, the Consciousness Project has had one overriding theme: the dynamic struggle between fear and love. As creatures struggling with the contradictions of conscious awareness, do we yield to our fears, run away, lash out in self-protective fury? Or do we confront our fears, and allow ourselves to be vulnerable? Do we dare to love, and unconditionally give?

When the other person is one's child, love, more often than not, triumphs over fear. When it is a workplace colleague, a neighbor of different color or ethnicity, or a citizen of another country or continent, fear, more often than not, triumphs over love.

Will we—alone and together—learn to treat one another as one another's children before we all perish?

QUESTIONS TO ASK, THINGS TO DO

Conscious Giving

Whenever you give a gift—and it need not be a material thing; it can be a word, a glance, or a smile—try inwardly pausing and asking yourself, "What is the quality of this act of giving? Is it truly unconditional? Is there that subtle inward sense of release, expansion, and joy that are the sensations that accompany the widening of the self? When you interact with your child, what quality of the heart are you conveying to them? We cannot rely on the words we speak, because children are more attuned to our tone of voice, the gentleness of our touch, the look in our eyes. Regardless of the interaction, whether you are praising or scolding them, is your love clear to them and to you? Or is there a feeling of constriction, of narrowness and tension, which are indications that the collar of fear is holding you back?

Children are our best teachers in this regard, because they have such remarkably sensitive antennae for receiving love, and are so difficult to fool.

Children, if we let them, can teach us how to love, and if we already know how, can help us improve. This is their gift to us, and perhaps the greatest reward of the Parent's Work.

Chapter 15

THE LEARNER'S WORK

❧

WHEN CHAO CHOU, a Buddhist monk of ninth-century China, was about to set out on a long pilgrimage, he said, "If I meet a child of three who has something to teach me, I will learn from him. If I meet a man of a hundred who can learn from me, I will teach him." Chao Chou was sixty years old at the time and already a respected religious figure. He could have simply said, "I have trained all my life as a Buddhist monk. It is now my responsibility to pass on what I have learned." Or he could have said, "Even though I am sixty, I have much to learn. I am still a student."

However, Chao Chou did not see his role as defined by either his age or his station in life, but by his situation. If the situation called on him to be a teacher, he would teach. Conversely, if he saw an opportunity to learn, he would jump wholeheartedly into the role of Learner. He didn't care about his status as a famous Buddhist teacher or what other people thought about him. All he cared about was the opportunity to keep learning.

It is said that Chao Chou lived to be one hundred twenty. We might wonder whether there was any relationship between his amazing longevity and his learning spirit. Today neurologists tell us that when we are challenged to learn, our brains continue to manufacture neurons well into old age. This finding surprised the researchers; it had long been thought that the brain couldn't do that. It seems that science is finally catching up with something the ancients such as Chao Chou already knew. Learning—whether worldly or spiritual—can continue as long as life does.

∞

Chao Chou spoke of "a child of three." Consider the energy, persistence, and curiosity of a child that age. Clearly, the Learner's Work is our first work. Never again will we be as dedicated and single-minded about learning as when we are young children. No one pays us to do this; our parents don't have to scold or cajole us. That comes later, once school begins and our innate curiosity is replaced by a more institutionalized form of learning. When very young we are voracious learners by nature.

There was a time—before reading and writing, grammar school, high school, and college—when this natural learning evolved into youthful apprenticeship and adult mastery. Without formal schooling, the child grew to maturity and joined the community of able-bodied adults. Even as recently as the Middle Ages, only priests and children of nobility attended any kind of school. Now it is taken for granted that the years from five to eighteen (or twenty-two) will be spent in formal schooling. This has become our first job.

Alana, a twenty-five-year-old medical student, had this to say about her years of formal schooling and the difficulties of that "job":

"I went through all those years of high school and college with no real idea of what I was doing or what I wanted to do. It was just what everyone did. In the back of my mind there was always this question, 'What am I going to be when I grow up?' But school wasn't about looking at that. It was just about passing tests and taking exams and trying to get into a good college, as though somehow that was enough and the career thing would work itself out later. It wasn't until I spent some summers in poor countries and saw how little people had in life, how much their basic needs weren't being met, that I decided I wanted to become a doctor."

Formal schooling taught Alana the skills needed to function in a knowledge economy, but not necessarily the perspective and experience for her to decide how to apply her skills. In fact, all the energy she had to put into taking exams and climbing the educational ladder may have obscured her inclination and natural gift as a healer.

THE LEARNER'S WORK IN CHILDHOOD

In today's world, we see formal education as a prerequisite for the good life. The uneducated live at the margins of society, capable of only minimum-wage employment, unable to fully integrate into a knowledge-based world.

Education begins in kindergarten, and sometimes sooner, as parents jostle to enroll their two- and three-year-olds in the right nursery schools, where children who are barely toilet trained are encouraged to begin sounding out letters and words, against the advice of many child-development specialists. In order to compete, so the thinking goes, our children must start early.

Whether all of this formal learning really produces the desired result is hard to say. In the article "When Backyards Were Laboratories," Henry Fountain speculates that many of our best inventors and engineers got their start with chemistry sets, ham radios, and other artifacts of a more leisurely, less structured childhood. Similarly, Anna Quindlen, in her essay "Doing Nothing Is Something," laments the loss of downtime among American children, a time for "open windows, day trips to the beach, pickup games, hanging out." How did this happen? Quindlen asks.

"Adults did it," she says. "There is a culture of adult distrust that suggests that a kid who is not playing softball or attending science-enrichment programs—or both—is huffing or boosting cars: If kids are left alone [so this thinking goes], they will not stare into the middle distance and consider the meaning of life and how come your nose in pictures never looks the way you think it should, but instead will get into trouble."

Henry Fountain contends that some of our best modern inventions germinated outside of a structured setting, and Quindlen concurs. There is certainly a role for formal schooling, and certain skills—the kinds tested on the college SATs—lend themselves to that kind of instruction. But if we think that formal schooling is all there is to learning, if we stop learning when formal schooling ceases, then a whole world of knowledge—both worldly and spiritual—passes us by. Quindlen implies that the "play" of childhood is an equally important form of learning. "Perhaps," she says, "it is not too late for American kids to be given the gift of enforced boredom for at least a week or two, staring into space, bored out of their gourds, exploring the inside of their own heads." Not too late for children, or for that matter, adults.

In fact, the kind of learning that comes from "fooling around," following our curiosity and inclination, happens throughout life, and may be the kind of learning for which our psyches are best adapted. Trial and error, imitation and intuition, are the way human beings have learned nearly everything for nearly all of our history. Certainly there is a place for structured learning, but it seems to work best when it is an adjunct to the "real" learning, and doesn't attempt to take its place. This applies to spiritual learning as well, as we shall presently see.

⌘

Childhood is a time when we learn how to learn. If our experience of learning is positive—and particularly if we discover the knack of learning on our own, without a curriculum to guide us—that knack carries into adult life. Adults who know how to learn, and who enjoy learning, keep learning throughout their lives, and, like Chao Chou, are willing to learn from anyone—even a three-year-old.

LIFELONG LEARNING

Gabe was a lifelong learner. A conscientious objector during the Korean War, he fulfilled his obligation by teaching English first in Palestine and then in Beirut, where he became familiar with Middle Eastern culture. In the 1960s, he apprenticed himself to the photographer Minor White and became a well-known photojournalist chronicling the civil rights movement in the American South. When his children were teenagers, in order to give them a different kind of schooling, Gabe and his wife, Jennie, bought a forty-two-foot sailboat and sailed across the Atlantic with their family.

Much later in life, Gabe took up skiing. He spent every winter on the slopes, becoming more and more adept, until one day he collided with a tree and broke his hip. During his year of recuperation, he had a long time to reflect. Realizing that his life as an expert skier might be over, and unwilling to resign himself to a sedentary life, Gabe, now seventy-two, decided that once he recovered he would learn to fly.

A few months after he finally earned his solo glider pilot's license I asked him about his lifelong propensity to try new things. He said, "I've had a lot of time to reflect on my style of working and learning. I realize I'm very process-oriented. What interests me in learning a new task or skill is the learning process itself, mastering the tools and skills. The goal, I think, becomes secondary. In fact, I find I start to get a little bored if I don't have that challenge and risk of learning something new. That was true even back when I was in the Middle East as a teacher, and certainly true when I was learning to become a photographer, and then a sailor and skier. I even took up welding at one point, just to get the sense of mastering the skill of working with metal."

"You broke your hip skiing," I said, "and yet while you were still recovering you decided to learn gliding. Wasn't that kind of foolhardy, at your age?"

"Maybe," he said. "But I wanted to get back on the horse, as they say. All my life I've had dreams of flying. It was a miracle I wasn't killed in that ski accident. It was a gift. If I wasn't going to learn to fly now, when would I ever? Besides, those skills—having to make quick judgments, the adventure of confronting the natural elements and the wind—are connected in my mind with a love of motion and a sense of staying young."

Gabe is a good example of an adult who is able to learn "outside the box." He has built his life around the principle that a willingness to keep learning is more important than the subject matter. Even when there is an academic form of the same subject—Gabe could have learned about Lebanon in a college history class, for example—learning from experience is best.

Learning a musical instrument is one example of a skill that can be taught both ways. It can be taught in academic fashion—first learning to read music, then playing scales, then exercises, then simple pieces, and so on. This is not a bad method for learning to play Mozart. But jazz musicians do not learn that way, nor do folk musicians all over the world. Such musicians learn to play by ear—much the way children learn their native language.

There are some aspects of music that can never be taught the academic way. Music is ultimately a language of feeling, and if the feeling isn't there, the music might as well be played by a computer. As a young man, I studied piano intensively. After I had mastered the essentials of technique, my piano teacher guided me mostly by metaphor, if he used words at all. "Like a storm cloud coming in," he would say, and if I didn't understand, he would brush me aside and sit down at the piano bench to demonstrate. "Like this!" And I had to hear the thunder cloud in his playing, and then find it in my own heart to turn the notes into the real music.

STAGES OF THE LEARNER'S WORK

The learning necessary to be fully human—our Whole Life's Work—progresses in three stages: childhood, adulthood, and spiritual maturity—or, as a Buddhist might say, Buddhahood. Just as there are formal and intuitive ways to learn language, skiing, or sailing, there are different methods for spiritual learning as well. The Western world was first introduced to Buddhism in the 19th century, through academic German and English translations of essential scriptures. D. T. Suzuki's series of *Essays on Zen Buddhism* in the 1930s introduced the theory, though not the practice, of Zen. It was not until the 1960s that Asian Buddhist teachers from the various meditation traditions arrived in the West to begin teaching the living, oral tradition.

Even within the living tradition there are various schools and styles. At one extreme are the detailed prayers, meditations, and visualizations of the Vajrayana tradition of Tibet. At the other extreme is the "just sitting" tradition of Zen. The Vajrayana way is more like learning music academically—reading music, practicing scales, understanding harmonies and chordal progressions. The Zen way is more like jazz; the instructions, to the extent that there are any, are general and vague. "Just sit"; "pay attention to what is going on in the body and mind"; "let thoughts come and go." The Vipassana tradition, dominant in Southeast Asia, lies somewhere in between.

Followers of these traditions may feel that there is some essential difference between them. But just as classically trained musicians often end up as masterful improvisers, and jazz musicians may attend music conservatories to learn the theory behind their improvisations, each of these schools of Buddhist-wisdom teaching incorporate aspects of the others. Gary Snyder, interviewed in *Conversations, Christian and Buddhist* back in the late 1960s, compared the Tibetan and Zen ways as follows:

"One proceeds in Zen by going directly to the ground of consciousness, to the contentless empty mirror of the mind, and then afterward, after ten or fifteen years of koan study, coming up bit by bit, using each of the koans as an exploration of those realms of the mind, having seen the ground of the mind first. The other, Tibetan Buddhism, works by the process of ten or fifteen years of going down bit by bit, till the ground of consciousness is reached, and then coming up swiftly. So that ultimately they arrive at the same place, but the Zen method is the reverse of the Tibetan."

It may be that these methods developed in Buddhism to accommodate people's different learning styles. Some people, like Gabe, are improvisers and are more comfortable with the Zen way—going "directly to the ground of consciousness." Others may prefer the more structured approach—"going down bit by bit." Since the destination is the same—a fully realized, mature human being, a Buddha—it matters less what method is used, and more that one stays with it all the way to the end.

Chao Chou's Learner's vow—"If I meet a child of three who has something to teach me, I will learn from him"—is an inspiration to us all. Chao Chou is considered one of the greatest Zen masters of China, and yet at the age of sixty he did not imagine that he had arrived or that his spiritual learning was finished. He understood that we are never finished, that being fully awake is not destination but something fluid, always in motion. It is those of us who haven't yet fully grasped this principle who think we have arrived. When learning stops, we think, This is me, I am an adult, I have arrived, I know things. When learning resumes, we abandon such notions and begin to move through life with delicacy and grace, understanding that whatever we think we know is not the whole of it. There is always something more, something unrevealed.

Childhood, adulthood, Buddhahood—it sounds like a college curriculum, with a before and after, and at the end a graduation. But from the standpoint of continuous learning, we could just as easily say, "Buddhahood, childhood, adulthood." The learning is a circle; we begin at the destination, or, as Lama Surya Das says, "We should not shoot the arrow at the target, but keep the target wrapped around the arrow as it flies."

❦

The outward manifestation of this attitude, as we see in Chao Chou's Learner's vow, is a transparent humility. The inner manifestion is what Shunryu Suzuki called "beginner's mind." Even a child of three can recognize these qualities in a person of deep cultivation; perhaps that was what Chao Chou was referring to when he spoke of learning from such a child.

Humility and beginner's mind: These are the inner work of the Learner, and the subject of the next chapter.

Chapter 16

THE LEARNER'S CONSCIOUSNESS: HUMILITY

CHILDHOOD, adulthood, spiritual maturity or Buddha-hood: These are the three stages of learning. Childhood is the time when we have the most natural energy for learning, when everything is fresh and new. When we are young we want to learn how to read, to ride a bicycle, to jump rope or throw a football. But the older we are, the more our curiosity shifts. We come to the point where we have mastered life's practical skills. We have had our share of joy and sorrow. The world, in all its commonplace triumphs and tragedies—the taste of a fresh melon, the passion of first love, the birth of a child, the death of a parent—has unfolded to us. At some point, perhaps in the face of some particularly grievous sorrow, the question may appear, as it did to Gauguin, "Where have we come from? Where are we going?" At this moment we stand in the vestibule of the path to Buddhahood. In this moment—which Buddhism calls *bodhicitta,* the thought of enlightenment—we have left ordinary childhood and even adulthood behind and have begun a new kind of search, in which each of us is a new kind of child, a spiritual child.

It is not necessary to be an older person to begin this work. The ultimate questions stand before us the moment we emerge from the womb. When we choose to confront them is only a matter of temperament and circumstance. Erik Erikson called this encounter—the last of his eight stages of man—the "integrity crisis." This crisis, Erikson says, usually comes to us later in life, when we come to reflect on our triumphs and regrets, and life's ultimate meaning. But it can come at any time. In *Young Man Luther,* Erikson explored Luther's spiritual awakening at the age of twenty, calling it a "premature integrity crisis."

Siddhartha Gautama had a similar experience when, at the age of twenty-nine, he left behind the palace, his princely life, and his responsibilities as a husband, father, and monarch-to-be, and sought the solitude of the forest to contemplate these universal questions. Like Luther, the thought of enlightenment had opened in Siddhartha's heart; he could not rest until he pursued it to the end.

Bodhicitta is not just another idea, not like the thought of a cherry milkshake. It is more like falling in love, though with a possibility rather than a person. And the spiritual Learner starts out in a state of natural humility, because nothing is known, and there is everything to learn, indeed like a new lover, or someone setting out to climb a mountain shrouded in mist. We must begin our climb not knowing the angle of ascent or the distance to the summit. Humility is easy at the beginning of such a trek, when we have nothing but questions. But as we go higher and further, and gain confidence—and particularly after we have some glimpse of the summit—that initial humility wanes. We begin to feel good about ourselves. We can conquer this mountain! And we are no longer beginners. We are experienced! And indeed, someone observing us might say, "Yes, this person is a good climber. He looks pretty good."

"Looks like good"—this was another of Shunryu Suzuki's favorite yet ungrammatical expressions. He was referring to people who seem skillful and accomplished on the outside. They do know something, or think they know something. Yet, inside there may be a problem. "Looks like good," taken by itself, is not a bad thing. It could be a compliment. We all know how hard it is to look good. Many of us don't look very good to ourselves or others much of the time. But "looks like good" can also be a trap, both in a worldly and a spiritual sense. It can mislead; it can result in betrayal and suffering, when the veneer comes off and "looks like" is gone. What is the difference between "looks like good" and "really good"? Sometimes it is nearly impossible to tell.

This is not a trivial matter. It is an important question, and the answer is not to be found in books. Not even a great master like Chao Chou could explain, although he gives us a subtle hint when he speaks of a child of three. This conundrum is worth hanging on the wall like a precious work of art and pondering for a long time. It doesn't yield its secret easily, but we can sense that it has something to do with humility, and its elusiveness. "Humility," said T. S. Eliot, "is the most difficult of all virtues to achieve; nothing dies harder than the desire to think well of oneself."

Humility is the inner reflection of the true Learner. If we do not retain a certain degree of humility in our lives, our minds will become closed—set in plaster, as William James said—and we will live out our lives coasting on old laurels rather than cultivating new ones. It is one thing if we are humble because we do not know much. In that case, humility is practical. We defer to our teachers partly out of self-interest. We want to know what they know, and we respect their ability to impart it to us. It is another thing to remain humble when, like Chao Chou, we are already accomplished, when we know much.

We know that humility is close to the essence of the spiritual life. At the same time, we can read in Buddhist meditation texts, for example, how much time and energy was devoted to the problem of pride. The authors of these scriptures lived in monasteries, having given up family, possessions, and all things of this world. Why then should pride—the opposite of humility—have been so much of a problem in these communities? Why is it that in Buddhism pride is considered one of the "higher fetters," those that persist even in spiritually developed persons, disappearing only in the highest stages of enlightenment? Clearly, from studying the texts, the answer is that an initial spiritual insight, an enlightenment, can become a powerful hindrance on its own. "I have it!" we think, and in that moment lose it. In fact, not only does spiritual pride grow in proportion to spiritual attainment, it is one of the last hindrances to be dissolved. Never does pride cling stronger than when we have something about which to be genuinely proud. And never does humility recede more quickly than the moment we say to ourselves, "At last! I have mastered it! There is nothing more to learn." As we continue to absorb the vast 2,500-year-old edifice of Buddhist teaching here in the West, this is an important lesson to keep in mind.

One day some of Beethoven's musical colleagues excitedly told him about a pianist, a rising young star in Vienna. "He's incredible!" they all said. "You must hear him." Beethoven was skeptical. This was not the first time he had been approached to confer his blessing on some young talent, and he was not easily impressed. But this time he went and heard the young man play. At the conclusion, Beethoven's colleagues anxiously awaited his verdict. "What do you think, Maestro?" they all asked. "Is he not wonderful?"

"He is very good," Beethoven finally replied. "But not good enough. His heart has not yet been broken."

Beethoven sensed that the young man's art was not yet complete. The youth was, perhaps, too taken with his ability, filled with pride in his gift and technique. Of course this was probably justified; without gift and technique, the pianist would not be good at all. But to be really great, to be able to convey the essence of the music, the pianist needed to go one step beyond, into an arena that had nothing to do with playing the piano or even with music—the arena of the heart.

This is the inner secret not only of artistic but of spiritual accomplishment. Perhaps that is why Chao Chou went on his pilgrimage at such an advanced age, and understood that even a three-year-old might have something to teach him. Perhaps, in spite of all his spiritual mastery, Chao Chou felt that his heart was not yet tender enough. He was willing—as so few of us are—to be a beginner over and over, until the very end.

∞

Shunryu Suzuki often talked about "beginner's mind." He was famous for it, and the title of his book *Zen Mind, Beginner's Mind* is well known among Buddhists. Yet, it is often misunderstood.

Beginner's mind doesn't have much to do with being a literal beginner. In fact, beginner's mind can be appreciated best by those who are not beginners.

Beginners do not need to work to experience beginner's mind; that is the nature of their minds, as expressed by the phrase "beginner's luck." We know intuitively that someone who has no preconceived idea of what to do—someone hitting a golf ball for the first time, or sitting down to do meditation—can often achieve something quite unusual. The golf ball may fly 250 yards that day, but it might take weeks or months of learning how to hit a golf ball before that moment of beginner's mind comes again. As Suzuki says, "In the beginner's mind there is no thought, 'I have attained something.' All self-centered thoughts limit our vast mind. When we have no thought of achievement . . . then we can really learn something. The beginner's mind is the mind of compassion."

Suzuki contrasts beginner's mind with self-centeredness and sees it as synonymous with compassion—a conclusion that may not be obvious unless one is immersed in the worldview of the Buddhist and understands that compassion is not just a charitable attitude but an outcome of a fundamental reorganization—an awakening—about who we think we are. The "vast mind" about which Suzuki speaks is not just a concept, it is a reality, a truth that we can experience and to which we can awaken.

"When we have no thought of achievement, we can really learn something." Easier said than done. How is it possible to have "no thought of achievement"? It sounds like a description of someone who is defeated or depressed. This is the paradox of humility, and of the Learner's Work. To learn as adults—to truly learn—we must simultaneously be of a mind like a young child and be fully cognizant of all that we already know.

This is why the ancient Buddhists agonized so much about spiritual pride, and why Suzuki's "beginner's mind" is such an advanced teaching. In another part of *Zen Mind, Beginner's Mind,* he described how professional calligraphers would practice making dots randomly on a piece of paper. Not so easy, he said. Inevitably the calligrapher would end up grouping the dots in some kind of recognizable pattern. To make the dots truly random, more than purpose or will was required. An "empty mind, a ready mind," said Suzuki, is required, a mind "ready for anything, open to anything."

This is the mind of humility and of the Learner's Work. In fact, the deepest form of the Learner's Work is not just to learn some particular thing but in the end to cultivate and develop such a mind. This is not childhood or adulthood but Buddhahood. Such work is not easy. "The most difficult thing," said Suzuki, "is always to keep your beginner's mind . . . it is the secret of Zen practice."

This understanding is not really a concept at all; it is a way to be and to live, one that all those who knew Suzuki experienced firsthand. Ed Brown, author, among other books, of *The Tassajara Bread Book* and translator/editor of Suzuki's *Not Always So,* described his first encounter with Suzuki this way:

I looked into his face, bowed, and then looked into his face again. He seemed very ordinary. His face was impassive, with no trace of liking or disliking, approving or disapproving. What did he think of me? Not a clue. I felt vaguely disquieted or unsettled, yet along with his impassivity was an uncanny quality of openness. I felt received. What was going on? How unusual, how strange: I was put off by his nonresponsiveness, yet blessed with acceptance. . . . Though his face showed no reaction I didn't sense that he was aloof or guarded or hiding what he must have been feeling, nor did I find him absent or somehow "not there." I had never met anyone like that—someone who seemed so completely present and receptive, yet unmoved on the surface, as though events reverberated and disappeared into some vast space. I felt grateful and privileged.

This is the face of the beginner's mind.

THE LEARNER'S WORK AND THE CONSCIOUSNESS PROJECT

We have based the notion of a Consciousness Project on the path of the Bodhisattvas, the beings who are willing to postpone their final awakening forever, if necessary, so that all other beings can be brought along with them. The ideal of Buddhahood, of spiritual perfection—like any ideal—has a flip side, or shadow. In this case the shadow is pride. Over the centuries Buddhism's ideal shifted from Buddhahood, with its notions of perfection, to Bodhisattvahood—a goal accessible to anyone. In its widest sense, we are all Bodhisattvas, all fellow toilers on the island of consciousness, cooperating, working together, caring for one another in an environment of like aspiration and shared fate.

The Bodhisattva is the spiritual Learner—never arriving, always working, letting others go first. This is the final resolution of the problem of spiritual pride, to cultivate beginner's mind forever, or, as Suzuki said, "When we have no thought of achievement, we can really learn something."

QUESTIONS TO ASK, THINGS TO DO

Are You an Expert?

Most of us are experts at something, whether it be pipe fitting, corporate finance, or gardening. These areas of expertise help define who we are. They give us confidence and balance those other areas of our lives where we may not do as well. Our expertise is a treasure, but without realizing it most of us come to depend on it for our very identity.

Suppose it were suddenly lost to you? Suppose you are a surgeon, and something happens to your hands? Suppose you are a professional athlete, and a car accident makes you unable to walk? You might think, Well, I'll deal with that when and if it happens. Until then, why worry about it? But, as Suzuki said, "All self-centered thoughts limit our vast mind." Our expertise can become a crutch, and even when we are healthy, it can make our spirits tense and narrow.

Ask yourself, "Suppose I were to lose my expertise, be unable to pursue my best skill—what would I do? Who would I be? Who would take care of me?"

This can become a personal meditation on the truth of impermanence and reveal how deep our cultivation of beginner's mind needs to go.

Where Is the Three-Year-Old Child?

When Chao Chou said, "If I meet a three-year-old child who can teach me," he wasn't referring literally to a young child but to anyone or anything that could give him an opportunity to grow.

Where is the three-year-old in your life? Is it your boss at work, whose unreasonable demands make your life so miserable? Is it your young child, perhaps? Is it your spouse, partner, or lover?

The world is full of Chao Chou's three-year-olds. As you go through your day, keep your eyes out for these serendipitous teachers. And when you are confronted with a difficult or challenging situation, you can say to yourself, "This situation is my three-year-old. It has come to me so that I can be a Learner again."

In this way you can refresh that sense of being the eternal beginner, over and over.

Chapter 17

THE ELDER'S WORK

❧

BEFORE THE DAYS of books and writing, of computers and the Internet, the totality of knowledge—where the best hunting grounds were, what plants were good to eat, when it was safe to cross the river and when not—was held by Elders, those who had lived long enough to accumulate an understanding of all these things. Even as recently as the eighteenth century, it was possible for a learned man such as Thomas Jefferson to have in his library nearly all the important literature and scientific knowledge then known. Then it was the job of the Elder to impart these things to the younger generation. This was the Elder's Work.

Today, the common store of all human knowledge is far more vast than any one person can master. No longer is important knowledge the exclusive purview of Elders. In fact, the retrieval of knowledge and the mastery of the new cybernetic tools are now much more the domain of the young, who take to computers and the Internet as though these recent inventions have always been. When it comes to knowledge, the Elders of today are more likely to be narrow specialists. A seventy-year old heart surgeon who has performed thousands of surgeries can be an invaluable resource to younger surgeons just learning their craft. But that older surgeon would not have had the time—as Thomas Jefferson did—to learn thirteen languages, master the Greek and Roman classics, study architecture and horticulture, serve as president, and invent an encryption machine in his spare time. Indeed, in the last few centuries, there has been a revolution in the acquisition, storage, and transmission of knowledge.

Wisdom, however, is another matter. Wisdom is not about the acquisition of skills or the memorization of facts. Wisdom's domain lies in another direction. It is not about knowledge but about experience, and in this arena the young must still defer to the old, because however brilliant or quick the young may be, they have not *lived*. While our knowledge explosion has given us space shuttles and CAT scans, Styrofoam and Prozac, when it comes to the essentials of human life—knowing how to love, how to raise strong, healthy children, and how to resolve conflicts between individuals, peoples, and nations—it is unclear how much progress we have made since ancient times. Knowledge is the hare of our world, racing ahead faster than we can keep up; wisdom is the tortoise, moving much more slowly. Wisdom moves slowly because it takes lifetimes to acquire, and there are no shortcuts. In fact, it is a perverse quality of wisdom that the faster we try to master it, the slower it comes to us; the very act of striving, as though for a college exam, can inhibit the receptive, intuitive quality of lived experience from blossoming. Wisdom remains the purview of the Elders among us, and the knowledge explosion has not diminished our need for them; it has strengthened it.

THE ROLE OF THE ELDER

Elders perform many roles in a society, as guides, mentors, and exemplars. But the most common form of the Elder's Work, ancient or modern, is to teach. Whether the teachers are younger or older, the basic role remains the same: to pass on what they know to their students. That said, not every teacher is a true Elder. To be both an Elder and teacher is a gift. These gifted teachers are the ones about whom we can later say, "This one truly inspired me, and set me on my life's course." We remember their confidence, their enthusiasm and generosity, and the way they inspired us and made us want to be like them. Diane, a college English professor, described her encounter with one of these special teachers:

"Mr. Brindley was my English teacher in my senior year of high school. The class was called English Honors. Only the brightest kids got in, and it was a real feather in one's cap to be accepted. Mr. Brindley made anything we read come alive, and he taught us how to have vigorous debates, to probe, to question everything. He was way too brilliant for high school. I wonder if he used to be a college professor who ended up in high school for some reason.

"We studied an enormous amount of material that year: all the world's major epics and religions, Greek tragedy, Shakespeare, T. S. Eliot, Dante's *Inferno*, Milton's *Paradise Lost*. That was where I got my first introduction to a thing called Zen, where monks sought enlightenment and hit each other with sticks. It was a roller-coaster ride through the high points of the world's great literature and wisdom, and Mr. Brindley was determined to stuff it all into our heads somehow, and make us think deeply about it to boot.

"I don't know what happened to Mr. Brindley, but if it weren't for him I would not be where I am today. He was more than an English teacher. He showed us how to think and live with real intensity and commitment, and how to transmit that to others. He was a teacher's teacher. Even today I don't think I am as good as he was in that way."

In listening to Diane describe Mr. Brindley, I got the sense that there was more to his story. I put this theory to Diane, who replied, "I never thought about it that way, but you're probably right. He lived by himself in this big old house, and once a school year he would invite us all out there for a party. There was something sad about him. He never talked about his own family, or whether he had ever had one. It was more like we were his family, and he wanted to do everything he could for us."

Clearly, Mr. Brindley was teaching something more than the curriculum. Mr. Brindley's gift had something to do with character, values, and a love of learning. And beneath all of that there was his way of being in the world—his life's wisdom. Though his official job title was English teacher, Mr. Brindley's actual function touched on something deeper. He may not have been an archetypal "wise man," but there was certainly something of the Elder in him.

BEING OLD AND BEING AN ELDER

To grow old is biological destiny. But to be an Elder implies something more, an inner attitude that transcends mere aging. The Elder is a person who knows about *things that matter*. The Elder is well versed in things that younger people might not know—not because they are not as smart or well educated but because they have not lived as long. And though we associate the state of Elder with old age, the Elder's Work can occasionally break through at any time. When a small child asks, "Who made God?" that is an unsettling moment for us. How do we answer? The question is so big, and suggests so much, that we aren't quite sure what to say. In the next moment the child skips off to her games, the question forgotten, and the Elder's moment is gone. But for a moment the sky opened, and we remember the big questions that once puzzled us, too. The very young share with the very old a proximity to the two events that ultimately define us all—birth and death. The very young have just come into the world; the very old are about to leave it. Those of us in the middle tend to forget that there was a time when we were not, and a time when we will again not be.

With the passing of traditional, extended families and communities, Elders are more and more being relegated to places apart—retirement communities, assisted living facilities, convalescent homes. No longer do we expect Grandfather and Grandmother to grow old in the company of family and a new generation of young children. This is unfortunate, because they have something to impart to us. They have been to school and to war, have had spouses and children. They have struggled with livelihoods and careers, been ill, seen loved ones leave or die, and grown old—"the full catastrophe!" as Zorba the Greek put it.

That being said, not every person of advanced years knows how to transform his or her raw experience into wisdom. Not every wizened person is wise. Not every grandparent is a font of wisdom. In the Elder's Work, as with any other, there is a range of capability and talent. All the more reason why those among us who are truly able to be Elders are so important, for they have a critical role to play in the transmission of culture and core values. Also, we younger ones must know how to listen to the tales; they may not be told in the ways we expect.

I found this out for myself when I spent some time with Rachel, a frail though sprightly woman of one hundred five. I started out by admitting to her that I—a mere youth of fifty-five—was somewhat intimidated by her advanced years, but she just laughed. Her age didn't seem that special to her, although she admitted to being surprised sometimes that she was "still here." Rachel had been a social studies teacher when she was young and had spent her later years—until she was in her nineties—as a master weaver. Thinking I might learn something about her long experience in this craft, I asked, "What do you think weaving has taught you?" But Rachel didn't seem to like this question; she demurred, and soon the conversation went on to other things.

It was only later, when she began taking me around the house, showing me examples of her work—tapestries of shore birds, a cabin in the woods, geometric abstractions, and one delicate bobbin-lace rendering of a young girl at play with two deer—that I began to understand. In the way her face lit up as she took me from room to room, showing me each piece and explaining what had inspired her to do it and how she had made it, I saw that the answer to my question was not some philosophical or spiritual abstraction. When she picked up a cotton placemat she had made, inspired by one she had seen during a tour of Monticello, and pointed out to me the intricate variations in the eighteenth-century pattern of the weave, I watched her hands, which were gnarled and veined from more than a century of use. I saw the way she handled the cloth, and felt her devotion to a physical craft and fine attention to detail that we don't see in today's manufactured creations. What had weaving

taught her? She was not telling me; she was showing me, trans-
mitting in her own way the wisdom of her years.

∽∾

This transmission, in its fullness, has several parts. First, it is
one individual's life journey. Second, it includes a reflection on
the meaning of that journey. What's the point of it all? Rachel's
tapestries and placemats—her "collected works"—were one
form of answer to that question. Third, it is a specific instance
of what Buddhism calls "sickness, old age, and death." I
thought of asking Rachel about this, but as we continued talking, the question seemed unnecessary. She was one hundred
five—twenty years beyond the age that most of us hope to
achieve. She had been living with old age for so long that for her
it had become a gift, a second form of youth.

But for those of us who are younger, the usual attitude, especially in a society that worships youth and health, is to think of
these things as somewhere out there, off in the future, things
that we will deal with when the time comes. For Elders, the
time has already come, and their mere presence among us, with
their illnesses and their stories, can help us understand that the
longer we put off facing sickness, old age, and death, the harder
they will be to deal with when they come. This is especially true
of death. For the final task of the Elder's Work is to die, and if
possible to die well.

∽∾

All our miracle drugs, the laser surgeries, the face-lifts, and the
botox injections are focused on the preservation of youth.
High-tech medicine sees death as a kind of failure rather than

an inevitable and dignified terminus of a journey. The medical miracles are indeed marvelous. If some antiaging medicine were suddenly to double the human life span, who would not want it? Who among us would not want to live longer, to do more, to see more, to be around when the great-grandchildren are grown?

And yet a life well lived depends on our willingness to depart from it with dignity, and let others take our place. Our final job, should circumstance and capacity allow us to exercise it, will be to let others know what we have learned over the course of our lives, so that the larger mission of consciousness can advance. And yet where is the training, the guidance, the assistance for us to do this work? Where is there a postgraduate course in the art of dying that tells us what we need to do and how to do it? Trust our technologically fascinated and spiritually challenged society to leave the most important tasks to chance, the most critical work of all to happenstance.

Death comes in all shapes and sizes, as does the wisdom about the dying process. Sam is a practicing Buddhist whose vocation for many years has been hospice work. One afternoon I sat down with him to talk about his experience taking care of hundreds of dying people, and he explained how different and idiosyncratic the process is for each person. "What's the one thing they all have in common?" I asked.

His reply:

"I think it's about people being able to tell their story. Everybody has her story, and if we are alert to it, we can help it come out.

"Gracie was a good example of that. When she first came to our hospice she was inconsolable. 'I just wanna die,' she kept saying.

"I didn't know what to do with that, but finally, after she'd said it enough times, it occurred to me to ask, 'What do you think is better about dying?'

" 'At least I'd get out,' she said.

"I thought she was talking about the physical pain. But the more we talked, the more her real story came out. She told me the whole story about her fifty years of marriage to her husband, the way she took care of him, made his meals, put his clothes out. All their life she'd taken care of him. She couldn't imagine him taking care of her, of being a burden on him, being dependent on him.

"Finally I asked her, 'Have you talked to your husband about this?'

"No, she shook her head, she hadn't. She couldn't.

"I encouraged her to do that over the next few days. It took quite a while, but finally they had that conversation. I wasn't there when it happened, but the upshot was that she moved out of hospice and lived another six months in the care of her husband."

Gracie's story was not so much about particular details of her life but about issues that are universal to all of us, such as loss of independence, and what those close to us might think of us in our infirmity—the feeling of "I don't want you to see me like this!" Gracie's wisdom was not some exalted thing, just the realization that she didn't have to "get out," that her situation could be all right, even though she was dying. Her husband would take care of her. Such a simple thing!

Another pattern that Sam mentioned was the way in which the dying person needs to give a gift. "Keep your eyes open," Sam said, "and it will happen every time."

"What do you mean, a gift?" I asked.

"It could be anything," Sam replied. "Sometimes it's a material thing, sometimes it's symbolic. And it's not the gift itself, but the process of transmission, the experience of passing something on. The important thing is that someone has to be there to receive it."

"Can you give me an example?"

"Well," Sam said, "there was Sally. She gave me her milk-glass collection."

This was a new one for me. "Milk glass?"

"Yep. Milk glass. It's a kind of glass. At one point she told me she had a collection, and I said, 'Gosh, that's funny, my mother had one too.' It was a fifties thing, I guess, housewives collecting different kinds of milk glass. And a few days later Sally said to me, 'I want you to have my collection.'

"For a while I couldn't figure that out. Why give it to me? After I thought about it for a while, I remembered that Sally had never had a child. I figured that this was some kind of mothering act, her finally getting to live out being a mother. And it wasn't just for her benefit, either. I got something out of it too—something a lot more profound than milk glass. It was very simple, but very touching, too."

In a world where death often occurs out of sight, we have all kinds of notions about death's significance. But Sam, who has been death's close companion for many years, has a much more down-to-earth view. He said, "The idea that some wonderful wisdom is going to come out of the dying process, or that people who are dying automatically become wise, is a kind of romantic notion, I think. Sometimes it's that way, and sometimes it isn't. The wisdom comes in all shapes and sizes, and the best way to understand it is just to observe it, watch whatever happens. Watching the process evokes our wisdom, both for the person dying and the caregiver." Giving a stranger her milk-glass collection: This may seem a mundane thing, but clearly it was not. The wisdom of one's dying moments emerges in its own fashion and takes its own form. We may not understand it, but we must respect it for what it is and can mean.

Sally and Gracie conveyed the wisdom of their dying in ways that made sense to them, through gift and story. The meaning of their passings emerged in how each one made peace with her life. Each offered her unique expression of the larger truth of things that embraces us all.

The wisdom traditions of the world, such as Buddhism, have made this larger truth their central topic of inquiry. This is the subject of the following chapter, which explores the inner dimension of the Elder's Work.

Chapter 18

THE ELDER'S
CONSCIOUSNESS:
WISDOM

❧

ONE OF SHUNRYU SUZUKI'S favorite phrases was "things-as-it-is." He was probably referring to the Sanskrit term *tathata,* which scholars usually translate as "suchness," or "thusness"—one of the many Buddhist terms pointing to the ground of Being. On occasion Suzuki's students would correct his grammar, saying, "No, Suzuki Roshi, it's things as *they are.*" He would try it out a few times—"things as they are, things as they are"—but in a few minutes would revert to his own way: things as *it is.* He wanted an expression that contained both plural and singular, the many and the one.

The phrase *things-as-it-is* expresses the unity between the things of this world in their infinite variety, and the is-ness that underlies it all and yet is not different from it. This Being is also the deepest stratum of who we are, the place out of which we emerge at birth and to which we return at death. And yet all during our lives we are not separate from it; and as wisdom grows with the passing of years, we may become more and more intimate with it.

When Suzuki was dying—bedridden with cancer and in great pain—one of his disciples visited him in his room. "Where will I meet you?" the disciple asked. Suzuki's tiny, frail hand came up from beneath the covers and made a circle in the air. In Zen, the circle represents our deepest nature. In Buddhist texts this is often referred to as "emptiness," or "void," but these English words do not entirely do justice to the essence, which has a quality of warmth and nourishment—a sense of "everything is all right." As Suzuki said in *Not Always So,* "Fading away into emptiness can feel like being at our mother's bosom, and we will feel as though she will take care of us."

Suzuki's circular gesture was a poignant example of the Elder's Work by a man who had spent his whole life in its study. He was saying, without a word being spoken, that he knew where he was going, just as Socrates, the archetypal wise man of the West, said to his grieving disciples when he was dying, "Why are you crying? I know where I am going."

It is rare to find Elders as accomplished as Socrates and Suzuki. But just as everyone who plays the piano can make a sound, every Elder has something to offer—even if only a fragment or snippet—of life's deepest and final wisdom. This deepest wisdom is what Suzuki was pointing to when he drew a circle in the air. This is *prajna paramita*—the "wisdom beyond wisdom"—the central topic of all of Buddhism, some might say of all religion. To be with a person at the final moments of their life, to see the breathing stop, the life drain from the face and limbs, and the whole life's history of the person fade away and the physical body shift in an instant from a pulsing organism to a lifeless husk already beginning to decay—this is the fundamental meditation, and the primal question. In every culture, in every generation, this fundamental meditation is renewed, the primal question is once again asked.

Forty years ago the spirituality shelves in bookstores were sparsely stocked. Now they are filled to overflowing. We are looking outside the traditions of our culture for guidance in this work. Words like *guru, sensei, roshi, rinpoche, kahuna, shaman,* and *lama*—along with the spiritual traditions they represent—have now entered our language. *"Birth and Death is the Great Matter"*—a traditional Zen saying—has become the spiritual rallying cry of a new generation that has been on the lookout for various kinds of *sensei*—a Japanese word that means literally "born before"—not only because they may be wiser but because they represent that part of ourselves that wants to be wiser. When we apprentice ourselves at the feet of the *sensei,* we are opening ourselves to our own higher nature, the Elder that is always in us.

This higher nature is the realm from which Socrates can say to his disciples, "I know where I am going," and Suzuki can lift his frail hand over his chest and make a circle in the air. This form of the Elder's Work naturally unfolds as we become old, but the work can occur any time, whenever the thought to explore the Great Matter occurs to us. In some who are spiritually inclined, or whose life circumstances predispose them to such searching, this thought occurs when young. Erik Erikson, in *Young Man Luther,* termed this youthful confrontation with the Great Matter—more properly the domain of the aging adult—a "premature integrity crisis." In Erikson's view, the integrity crisis is the last developmental challenge of our psyches. To come to "integrity," as he uses the word, is to make peace with the lives we have lived and the end that is to come.

But an earlier crisis of integrity is premature only in the sense that it is driven by a conscious desire to understand where we are going. In this wider sense, the Elder's Work is always going on, well beneath the surface in most individuals, and roiling on the top in those so inclined. There are times in history when the crisis of integrity becomes the domain not just of a few but of the many. In the ancient societies of India and Greece the spiritual search was honored as life's highest calling. We may be seeing a resurgence of this attitude in our time and place, which seems particularly estranged from the Great Matter, with our fascination with game shows, hamburger ads, and the need wear the right shade of lipstick or the cool athletic shoe. These trivia are the shiny skin of our new postindustrial life, where youth is everything and distraction rules. But the stubborn truths of "sickness, old age, and death" are never far. Death remains our first and best spiritual teacher, and the more MTV blares at us with images of youth and sex, the more Death beckons as a counterpoint.

According to Buddhism, death teaches us three basic facts about life: that all we hold dear will inevitably pass away, that our own separate identity is but a temporary, shimmering construct, and that life is *dukkha,* a complex term usually translated as "suffering," though it actually means the fundamentally tragic undertone to both joy and sorrow. These three "marks of conditioned existence"—impermanence, the illusory nature of the self, and the fact of human suffering—come across to our modern sensibility as rather bad news, particularly now that we have the technology and medical knowledge to postpone these facts of life for a long time. But Buddhism does not view these three truths as either good news or bad. They are simply "things as it is," and that being so, far better for us to accept them and learn to live with them than to push them off and deny them until it is nearly too late. But how can we truly accept them? How can we live full lives in accordance with these principles?

Impermanence. Yes, it is true that everything we cherish is destined to pass away. But accepting the fullness of this truth in the way we live need not be sad. When we see every person or thing like delicate flowers nodding in the wind, their petals already beginning to drop off, we come to appreciate them all the more. At that moment, love opens in our hearts for the gift of being alive, and when tears come they are not of sadness but of joy.

No Abiding Self. Once we see the self as only a tentative construction, and experience its basic wispiness, a whole lifetime of guardedness falls away, and a deeper freedom emerges. Dr. Seymour Boorstein, in discussing the way that proximity to death can free us from the narrow bounds of self, put it this way: "Often when one approaches death and its certainty with acceptance and resignation, there is revealed a lovingness that neurotic, emotional defensiveness previously covered over. At this time, our defensiveness no longer serves a purpose since death is happening RIGHT NOW—rather than at some unspecified date in the future—and our basic loving nature is revealed."

Suffering. Yes, it is true that all that we love and care about will eventually pass away and that life is, in the end, fundamentally tragic. But this is not just a bad thing. Tragedy opens us to the richness of life's tapestry in a way that distraction or comedy cannot. The tragedies of Shakespeare are considered his greatest plays. It is from these that his most-quoted lines come, not because the comedies are not also great but because the tragedies reverberate more deeply with the truth of "things as it is." From comedy comes a passing enjoyment. But from tragedy comes a different sort of joy, deeper than ordinary pleasure or pain, the joy of being thoroughly alive, all of us struggling together in the middle of it all.

Our new century provides a cacophony of television images, blaring music, recreational sex and drugs, a never-ending menu of entertainments and distractions—all designed to paper over and disguise the tragic underbelly of life. We are on our way to perfecting an as-if world, a state of affairs that was predicted in 1932 by Aldous Huxley's *Brave New World,* a dystopian novel set in the distant future, where parenthood has been abolished, fetuses are raised in bottles, and all suffering is palliated by a psychedelic drug called soma. Early in the book, Huxley introduces the character of the Savage, a man raised on a New Mexico Native American "reservation." Until his sudden introduction to the futuristic society of London, the Savage's only exposure to the world outside his own has been two books: the Bible and the collected works of Shakespeare. He is repulsed by the superficiality of the modern world. In a conversation with Mustapha Mond, one of its leaders, the Savage listens while Mond explains that the modern world is based on comfort. The Savage replies:

> "I don't want comfort. I want God, I want poetry, I want real danger, I want freedom, I want goodness. I want sin."
>
> "In fact," said Mustapha Mond, "you're claiming the right to be unhappy."

"All right then," said the Savage defiantly, "I'm claiming the right to be unhappy."

"Not to mention the right to grow old and ugly and impotent; the right to have syphilis and cancer; the right to have too little to eat; the right to be lousy; the right to live in constant apprehension of what may happen tomorrow; the right to catch typhoid; the right to be tortured by unspeakable pains of every kind." There was a long silence.

"I claim them all," said the Savage at last.

Mustapha Mond shrugged his shoulders. "You're welcome," he said.

The Savage understood that only with a Shakespearean sense of tragedy does life become vivid and real; only then is real awakening possible. The "modern" world into which he had been thrust was an as-if world of fantasy and illusion; what he was claiming was not really a "right" to be unhappy—that was Mustapha Mond's interpretation of his view—but a hunger to be fully human, to embrace it all, to be complete.

The poet Lew Welch expressed a similar point of view in the poem *I Saw Myself:*

I saw myself
a ring of bone
in the clear stream
of all of it.

and vowed,
always to be open to it
that all of it
might flow through

. . .

and then heard
"ring of bone" where
ring is what a

bell does.

Welch vowed "always be open to it, that all of it might flow through." This is similar to the Savage's feeling when he said, "I want God, I want poetry, I want real danger, I want freedom, I want goodness." These passages express an attitude that embraces all of life, without reservation, without separation, with composure and courage. We can also sense in both the Savage and the Welch poem a sense of the tragic—Welch visualizes his body as already decomposing, as a "ring of bone"; the Savage "defiantly" claims the "right to be unhappy"—as well as deep compassion for the human state, not unlike the Bodhisattvas' openhearted resolve to embrace the fate of all beings as their own.

From Buddhist scriptures, with their elaborate descriptions of exalted spiritual states and celestial beings, we may think that a Buddha, or a Bodhisattva, is a perfected, unblemished being. But observing the living Buddhist teachers who have come to the West in the last half century, we get a sense that the goal is not so much perfection as *completeness*. To be a complete human being—fully conscious of the tragic quality of life that underlies all ordinary joy and sorrow, and of our own humanity and imperfection amid it, and yet vowing to stay with it, and be open to it—is a deeper and more substantive kind of realization than any idealistic vision of Buddhahood as an otherworldly spiritual perfection.

Dr. Boorstein described how, when near death, we can come to this openness and completeness, which he describes as a "lovingness that neurotic, emotional defensiveness previously covered over." Perhaps Buddhist teaching is a way of consciously bringing on this openness, and overcoming our "neurotic, emotional defensiveness," well before the near-death state. Buddhism's prescription for this process—long years of immersion in meditation and other spiritual practices—may be right for some, but even for those who are not inclined to Buddhism, or whose life circumstances do not allow them the time, life itself sometimes provides the path.

A serious illness is an example of a life experience that can precipitate this kind of breakthough. We often think of illness as an interruption in the orderly flow of our life, a misfortune to be overcome as quickly as possible. It certainly is a misfortune; no one likes to be ill. But illness can also be a great opportunity in a spiritual sense. The Buddhist meditations on the impermanence of the body, its inevitable decay, and the omnipresent fact of death hardly need to be performed at a time like this. The illness itself is the meditation.

Kevin, a successful businessman and active philanthropist, was forty-eight and the father of two small children when his car skidded during a driving rainstorm and collided with a telephone pole. He was in a coma for several days. When he opened his eyes, he couldn't recognize anyone. It was several weeks before his mental and physical functioning began to return, and nearly two years before he fully recovered. What was this like for him, I asked, particularly when he was in the coma, far from our world?

"I wasn't conscious, but I wasn't exactly unconscious either. It was as though I were floating in a pool of light. I didn't have a body. I wasn't me anymore. I didn't know who I was at all. But I had some kind of awareness. I wasn't frightened, or anxious. I didn't feel anything, really, except a kind of deep peaceful feeling. I tried a samadhi tank a few years back, the kind where you lie in a pool of warm salt water in complete darkness. The coma was kind of like that.

"Even after I woke up, I was still in that world. I could see my wife's face leaning over me. I both knew and didn't know who she was. I was still mostly in that pool of light, and it was like she had dipped her head into it so I could see her. It took a long time for that light to fade, and when it did, and I could finally see that I was in a hospital room, and began to understand what she was telling me, about the car accident and all, I remember feeling a kind of regret that now I would have to come back to the world and all its pain. It was only then that I began to feel scared."

"Now that you're all better, how has that experience changed you?" I asked Kevin.

He smiled a little sadly. "It's all fading now. I'm pretty much back to my normal life. But something is different. That light never went away completely. It's as though I can still see it a little bit, out of the corner of my eye. And I think I'm a little more patient with people—especially my children. That's what my wife says, anyway. Sometimes when I watch my kids playing out in the yard I feel like crying. It's all so beautiful, this world, and I came so close to leaving it. I don't think I'll ever be able to take it for granted again."

"So how do you feel about the accident now?"

"How do you mean?" he asked.

"Do you feel in some way it was a kind of gift?"

He laughed. "Two years out of my life, I went through such hell. Some gift!" Then he paused. "But some part of it was a gift, maybe. Maybe so." He shook his head, as though trying to clear away the painful memories. "Yeah," he said. "I'll buy that, that it was a gift. I sure wish there was an easier way, though."

It's tempting to put a label on Kevin's experience, to call it spiritual or life transforming. But Kevin himself was not comfortable with these ideas when I proposed them to him. He seemed more comfortable letting it remain nameless. "It's just what it was," he said.

And what was it? Death is the great mystery, the eternal conundrum, and we all have a fascination for near-death stories and the tales told by those who have returned from death's gate. But Kevin's story reminds us that even for those who have had such an experience, life goes on. The experience becomes yet another milestone in life's journey, not to enlightenment or spiritual perfection, necessarily, but to greater completeness.

WISDOM AND THE CONSCIOUSNESS PROJECT

There is a tendency to think of the Consciousness Project as some grand evolutionary design for the human race. In some sense it is, but that's not all it is. It cannot be some spiritual form of General Electric's old corporate slogan, "Progress is our most important product!" Neither is it some cartoon showing an amphibian crawling out of the surf and gradually morphing into a man with a briefcase and a business suit. Without Wisdom, without the interior aspect of the Elder's Work, the Consciousness Project will devolve into squabbling and quarreling, as competing visions of our destiny vie for supremacy.

The Consciousness Project can flourish only in the light of our common humanity, in humility and compassion for one another. When Suzuki's frail hand came out of the bed and he made a circle in the air, he was charting a course for all of us. When Huxley's Savage reclaimed all the richness and contradictoriness of human joy and suffering and rejected the artificial, plastic world of Mustapha Mond, he was returning to the roots of the Consciousness Project. Kevin, watching his children play outside with tears in his eyes, could be any one of us, touched by near-death and blessed with continued life.

Throughout this book the image for the Consciousness Project has been an island moving northward with painful slowness. It is tempting to imagine that somewhere, out in the vast ocean, there is an "other shore" on which we will finally arrive—at the end of our own life or at the end of countless generations. But the "other shore" is not out there. It is here. We are surrounded by it on all sides. Each breath, each footstep, each encounter with another human being, so much like ourselves, is the other shore.

QUESTIONS TO ASK, THINGS TO DO

Can You Be an Elder?

No matter what your age, no matter how much or how little you know about the matters discussed in the last two chapters, there may be a situation, circumstance, or relationship in which you can perform the role of Elder. Remember the second half of Chao Chou's vow: "If I meet a man of a hundred who can learn from me, I will teach him." The man (or woman) doesn't need to be a hundred. Perhaps she is five. Perhaps she is your own age. If your livelihood includes guiding or mentoring others—and many jobs do—think of including in your teaching role not only the skills and the facts but your demeanor, your attitude, your appreciation of the knowledge you have. Even if you are no expert, imparting your knowledge in a spirit of humility and sincerity will always be appreciated. If you lack confidence in what you know or in your ability to communicate it (this often comes up in connection with public speaking), be honest. One popular speaker dreaded every appearance. Finally he hit on a way to defuse his anxiety. He began every speech by saying to the audience, "Frankly, I'm terrified of what you will think of me. So please, all of you, smile. That will help." The audience didn't just smile, they laughed, which allowed them and the speaker to relax, and the teaching and learning to proceed in a spirit of mutual well-wishing.

When we are with children we can always be Elders, since they are so eager to learn. Taking time to nurture children will always bear fruit, as long as we realize that they too have a piece of the Elder's Work and can teach us at the same time as we are teaching them.

Chapter 19

A WHOLE LIFE'S WORK

❧

THE ARTIST NAOMI, whom we met in chapter 7, liked to compare our human life to an improvised theater piece, saying, "You only get one chance, you can't practice and you can't go back." Nevertheless, some people do their best to write a script. David, a computer operations manager, told me, "I'm twenty-eight now. By thirty I'm going to be a director. I want to make vice president by thirty-five, chief operating officer by forty. By forty-five I should have enough equity to cash out and retire."

Others plan a future for their families. "We've been married a year," Pamela said. "We want to have three kids, I hope two girls and a boy, though I think my husband would like two boys and a girl. One of them I know is going to be named Elizabeth, after my grandmother. We've already started a college fund for them."

Such neatly laid plans rarely come true in the way we imagine; for most of us, life really is like Naomi's improvised play.

There is not much about our life that we can really control. All of Buddhism's talk of impermanence, of "sickness, old age, and death"—messages that seem a bit morbid to read on the page—boil down to the simple fact that though we do our best to build a career, raise a family, and cultivate our passions, in the end we are at the mercy of luck and happenstance. Our hopes and dreams aside, our life is defined by the things that happen to us.

So when we speak of embracing our Whole Life's Work we are not referring to family or career. It is not even a matter of planning the accomplishments we would like to leave behind—our "collected works." When it comes to our whole life, we cannot treat it as though it were a well-planned construction project. Nor is life like a conveyor belt with a baby on one end and an elderly person at the other. Our Whole Life's Work is already here; it is all happening in the present moment.

It may seem as though the eight modes of work we have spent most of the book exploring exist in some linear sequence, but in reality they do not. They are not lined up in past or future, but exist right now, simultaneously. It is true that as we grow from child to adult to Elder, our way of doing these modes—their emphasis and proportion—changes. When we are young, the Learner's Work predominates. In midlife, it might be the Hobbyist's or the Creator's Work. When we are old, we take on the mantle of Elder. But when we speak of our Whole Life's Work, we are not speaking of the future. Embracing it means "becoming aware of" or "taking responsibility for." If our life is indeed a piece of improvised theater, then the eight modes of work are like eight characters who are always on stage, from beginning to end. We are each of these characters, as well as the director, the audience, and the theater critic. There is no time to write the play beforehand. We make it up as we go along. And the thing that most determines how the play will go—whether, at the end, the theater critic within us can say, "Not a bad play. All in all, pretty good"—is how conscious and directive we can be about what is happening on stage.

As we have seen in all the previous chapters, this improvisational theater piece operates on two fronts, an exterior one—the various modes of work—and an interior one of maturation and spiritual development. Spiritual traditions such as Buddhism have tended to see this inner work as needing to take place in a cloistered environment, apart from the hurly-burly of the world—in a monastery or retreat center or in the quiet of meditation and prayer. In contrast to this traditional view, we have been exploring the ways that the inner and outer can grow together—that in the very hurly-burly of life, and all the activities we pursue in it, there are myriad opportunities. This attitude toward the balance between inner and outer fits with the circumstances of our modern life, in which the monastery is not some place apart, but the place we are in. Our eight-fold schema of A Whole Life's Work is the playing out of this notion of the whole world as a monastery, of life itself as a retreat. This may seem radical, but actually it is not a new idea. We find it embedded in Buddhism's highest teachings.

The Buddhist scholar John Blofeld, when beginning a course of training under a renowned Buddhist master, was told to meditate on the following: "See everything around you as nirvana. See all beings as the Buddha. Hear all sounds as sacred." This instruction seems either trivial or profound beyond comprehension. We know that everything around is not perfect, not nirvana. All beings are definitely not the Buddha, especially not the road-rage specialist who just made an obscene gesture and cut us off on the freeway. And in what way is the sound of a garbage truck at 5 A.M. sacred?

Blofeld himself gives us an answer. Lama Surya Das visited

him in Thailand in the early 1970s; he described Blofeld's attitude this way: "At first the traffic noise bothered him during his morning meditations, but after a while he realized that the cacophony wasn't much different [except how he thought about it] than the cacophonous sound of morning *puja* [ritual] coming from his master's monastery at Kalimpong when he'd lived there during the fifties. Thus he got used to hearing the traffic noise outside the window of his home's Tara shrine meditation room as divine *puja* sounds instead of distracting, discordant interruptions from the modern world."

The Buddha taught that our minds are clouded by passions such as lust, greed, and anger, by foolish clinging to material possessions, and above all by a misunderstanding about the nature of the self. We do not understand, he taught, that everything is constantly changing, in flux, and destined to pass away, most especially our cherished identity as individual, separate selves. Because of this misunderstanding we continually fail, as individuals and as societies, to live in harmony with one another and with the wider living world.

We suffer, in other words, because we misunderstand the world in which we live, and the only way to escape this suffering is to fundamentally alter our understanding of it, by transforming the mind with which we perceive it. This work of transformation can be understood in two ways. In one way, the ordinary world, with all its temptations and distractions, is seen as an impediment to the path of liberation. This is the essence of the monastic life—to radically simplify one's existence so that we can observe the mind, hour by hour, day by day, for weeks, months, and years, without distraction. This way imagines the spiritual path as a linear process with a before and after: First we wander in ignorance, then we spend long years in concentrated spiritual study, after which we are able to achieve wisdom.

Another way to understand the worldly life, and the process of liberation, was expressed by John Blofeld's master when he said, "See everything around you as nirvana." This is to understand the worldly and the spiritual not as two but as one; the features of everyday life, with all its passions, distractions, and illusions, not as impediments but as opportunities; the work of spiritual transformation not as a path in linear time but as an eternal verity that arises in every moment. Penetrating this truth in all the various circumstances of our life, in each mode of work and the inner consciousness that is its corollary, is how we understand our Whole Life's Work.

There is a reason why all Buddhist traditions classify this understanding as the highest and most profound teaching—it is both tremendously challenging and easily misunderstood. Taken at face value, it sounds as though we needn't make any effort at all. "We're already Buddhas!" we can say. "Nirvana is here. Great. No need to work at it. Five minutes of meditation once a week should do it." This is like saying that in baseball there is no secret to hitting—just swing the bat! Ted Williams, probably baseball's greatest hitter, when asked what was the secret of his success, said just that: "See the ball, hit the ball."

Ted Williams could say that, just as John Blofeld's master could say, "See all beings as Buddha." For the rest of us (indeed for all of us—Ted Williams practiced constantly), there is a reason for the monastic life, for meditation retreats, for a lifetime of practices and prayers—to make this highest insight more than just an intellectual abstraction. But we may have come to a point in history where the whole notion of monastic life can be refashioned. Now that livelihood and survival do not require all our time, we actually may be able to imagine treating the whole world as our monastery, our whole life as a template for spiritual work, and its monastic aspects—individual time for retreat,

reflection, and meditation—not as an exclusive lifelong vocation but one of many modes of inner and outer work. To quote
Shunryu Suzuki on this point again (remembering that when
he says "priests," he means people who have committed themselves to full-time spiritual practice): "American students are
not priests and yet not completely laymen. I understand it this
way: that you are not priests is an easy matter, but that you are
not exactly layman is more difficult. I think you are special people and want some special practice that is not exactly priest's
practice and not exactly layman's practice. You are on your way
to discovering some appropriate way of life."

The eight stages of work can be seen as the exterior aspect of
this "appropriate way of life." The eight modes of conscious-
nesses—Precepts, Vitality, Patience, Calm, Equanimity, Giving,
Humility, and Wisdom—are the interior aspect, which others
cannot easily see. But these are in the end the most important. It
is not enough for our theater piece to look good from the outside, for us to pursue the eight modes of work only in their
exterior aspect. For the theater piece of our life to work, "looks
like good" is not enough. We have to dedicate our whole life to
making it real.

And as we do this, we must also remember that a somewhat
different version of this theater piece is being performed by
each person in the world, and that the plays are all connected.
They are actually all part of one enormous play—the Consciousness Project. These other improvisations on the theme of
life are not on our stage, but they affect everything we do, and
vice versa.

Thus we come to the final verse in the theater piece of life
and of our Whole Life's Work—the Consciousness Project.

Chapter 20

THE CONSCIOUSNESS
PROJECT

❧

THERE IS A CLASSIC science-fiction novel titled *Orphans in the Sky,* by Robert Heinlein. The book opens mysteriously. A group of young people are about to embark on a journey, a coming-of-age saga that requires them to climb a ladder through a hole in the sky. They do this and enter another, even stranger world. It is only gradually that the reader comes to realize that this mysterious world is in fact a spherical spaceship. The place the group began is but the outermost of four layers of the sphere. The spaceship has been traveling through space for generations. Nearly everyone—except the theoretical scientists who live in its core—has forgotten the original purpose of the journey. The inhabitants of each circle have each developed their own mythologies, their own genesis stories, and their own fears and prejudices about the inhabitants of the other layers.

But as the group of adventurers gradually climb deeper and deeper into the spherical ship, and finally meet the physicists in the center who alone understand the original nature of the mission, we come to realize that after traveling through the void for many hundreds of years, the spaceship is about to arrive at its destination—a habitable planet orbiting a distant star. The people in the ship are the target generation, the culmination of many lifetimes spent on the ship. If the inhabitants of the ship do not gain this knowledge in time, the spaceship will crash and the entire journey will have been for naught. They must learn the truth. That is their challenge.

We too are a kind of target generation. It has taken humanity all of its history to finally fill the spherical spaceship we call earth to overflowing. Invention, pollution, weaponry, and population have all reached their culmination in our time. We are the first generation whose home sphere could be destroyed by us, and for the same reasons as the fictional one—because we have forgotten who we are and why we are here. Just like the inhabitants of that fictional spaceship, we have constructed our own mythologies. Some of us may imagine that our highest purpose here is to be rich, or to be famous, or to convert the whole world to our religion. The problem is not that these stories conflict. Conflict in life is inevitable. The problem is the destructive capacity, or as Thich Nhat Hanh said, referring to his own ravaged country, "We Vietnamese fought each other with bows and arrows for thousands of years, but we survived; now that you from the West have given us guns and bombs, we may all fall."

Our crisis is not only of identity but of purpose. We need to be more awake, more aware, more compassionate, and more kind—but now not just because our religious teachings tell us that this is a good thing, but because if we don't, all may be lost.

We began our exploration of A Whole Life's Work by pointing out that our first purpose as living creatures is to survive. The eight modes of outer work—the Earner, the Hobbyist, the Creator, the Monk, the Helper, the Parent, the Learner, and the Elder—are the way we survive, the journey we take in the exterior world to develop ourselves fully and understand our rightful and fulfilling place in the world. These are how we pass on the fruits of our survival to the next generation.

But we now know that survival—even a fulfilling, fruitful survival—is not enough. The eight inner modes of work—Precepts, Vitality, Patience, Calm, Giving, Equanimity, Humility, and Wisdom—are equally important. In fact, now they are even more important. Developing our inner life, individually and collectively, is now critical to our survival, in a way it never was before. As the target generation, we now understand that survival and the Consciousness Project amount to nearly the same thing. Both the beast and the Buddha that dwell within us must learn to make peace with each other on the same ground as that which unites all the world's religions, the ground of compassion.

That compassionate ground may seem but a tiny voice in the world's cacophony of quarreling voices, but, like the power of gravity, in the aggregate it has great power. Compassion is the universal language of human relations. And beyond the human world, animals and even plants understand the difference between helping and hurting, between thriving and suffering. Those whose spiritual point of reference is the Koran, the Bible, the Torah, or the Bhagavad Gita also embrace the promise to work for the liberation and welfare of all beings everywhere in the world. Some people make the promise more paramount in their lives than others, but for the ordinary citizen, that promise is implicit in the interchange of daily life. We all have the seeds of compassion working in our hearts. Whether the seeds are dormant or fruitful, as long as the heart still beats, they are there.

THE COMPASSION WORKER

The mission of our Whole Life's Work is to exercise and express the Bodhisattva vow in whatever way we can. It does not matter whether we are Buddhists. To say, "However many beings there are in the world, I vow to liberate them all," is more fundamental than Buddhism or any other ism. In fact, the word *Buddhism* itself is an invention of scholars who needed an "ism" to contrast with other "isms." There is no such word within Buddhist teaching. The Buddha spoke only of the Path, and of awakening. Later generations of Buddhists spoke of the Bodhisattva.

And the Bodhisattva is, after all, a kind of worker—a compassion worker, we might say. The Bodhisatta's vow is not an abstraction, not a lofty ideal. The compassion worker is an active presence, and the eight modes of work and their interior virtues are nothing more than a description of the ways in which a compassion worker can function. Compassion workers can be bankers, fishermen, politicians, tax accountants. They could be soldiers, policemen, teachers, parents. They can be anyone with a wise and compassionate heart, regardless of job description.

In the widest sense we are all compassion workers. It is certainly true that not everyone outwardly manifests the qualities and behaviors of the compassion worker, but even saints are not saints 100 percent of the time. The vocation of the compassion worker happens by degrees, and the beginning stage, the novice rank, is simply to be born a human being, with the mind, feelings, and all the potential of a human being. To be compassionate, one must know compassion. And what human being is not responsive to an act of generosity or kindness? Even the homeless person on the street who curses us when we extend a helping hand, the ruthless dictator who despises any show of kindness as pathetic weakness, even the sociopath condemned to death for horrible crimes, reacts to a show of kindness with some spark of recognition. Even acts of mind-numbing cruelty, such as the Holocaust or the Soviet Gulag, have the paradoxical effect of moving the Consciousness Project closer to its goal by showing us how dark is the abyss of going backward. Our greatest evils, our most monstrous failings, have this one saving grace: They teach us the way we must not go, and therefore the way we have to go. How many have died to show us this way! One day we may fully understand and appreciate the sacrifices they have made on our behalf. But not yet. We have so much more to do.

No, not yet. In chapter 8, we told a story about "not yet." As we near the end of our exploration of *A Whole Life's Work*, it is a story worth repeating.

During a formal question-and-answer session a woman approached Shunryu Suzuki and said a single word, *"Mada."*

Suzuki sat up straight and replied in a loud voice, "Yes! *Mada* is very important. *Mada* means NOT YET!"

The experience of "not yet" is fundamental to the human situation and to spiritual learning. For the compassion worker, "not yet" means honesty and humility. It means that we are not finished, there is more to be done, more to learn, more to understand. The effort is continuous, ongoing. It doesn't matter how exalted our status, how prestigious our degrees, how deep our spiritual understanding. "Not yet" means just what it says. Our lifetime is short and full of detours and distractions. Things never work out the way we imagine. "Not yet" could mean a kind of regret.

But it is much more than that. "Not yet" is also the summation of the whole Bodhisattva vow, our Whole Life's Work, the compassion worker's mission. No matter how many more generations of humanity come and go upon the planet, it will always be "not yet." Why think of any goal, whether modest or world-encompassing, as final?

"Not yet" is the treasure of this world, and our common fate. Let us forgive one another, and work together, as much as we can. And be patient, too. In that regard, there is an old Buddhist saying that Suzuki loved, and which aptly describes his way of being in the world: "When you walk in the rain, do not hurry. It is raining everywhere."

FINAL WORDS

We have now come to the end of our exploration of A Whole Life's Work. We have seen how this work functions in eight modes and on many levels: in the individual and in all of humanity, in our outer work and interior consciousness. Though it has gone by many other names, we have chosen to call all of it the Consciousness Project. This project supposes that the whole history of humanity has been slowing, inching along—sometimes forward, sometimes back—toward greater conscious awareness, toward greater care and compassion.

Some might say that, like any idealistic vision, this one too is flawed. Human nature, these critics might say, is what it has always been—a volatile mixture of light and dark, positive and negative, earthly and divine. To read history in any other way, they say, is to impute more than is there, and to engage in wishful thinking. They may have a valid point. But it is not a question of whether our view or theirs is correct, or whether the Consciousness Project is a reality or wishful thinking. If there were a way to scientifically measure the project's existence, then it would simply be our destiny and not a project. But it *is* a project, about whose future there can be no certainty; it may succeed, or it may fail. Whether in the end our higher nature will prevail or we will succumb to the darkness that is still so prominent in our nature, we cannot say.

It is the question that all of us carry, for ourselves and for everyone, for as long as we live.

Let us, as Suzuki said, all walk in the rain with purpose and dedication, neither lagging behind nor rushing ahead.

It is raining everywhere.

ACKNOWLEDGMENTS

THIS BOOK HAS BEEN a collaboration of many souls—many voices, stories, and points of view. Among them, I would like to thank Susan Clarke, Julie Forbes, Riley Fulton, Matt Heron, Ruth Herron, George Lane, Marc Lesser, Frank Ostacewski, Bob Rogers, Bill Sterling, Millicent Tomkins, and Steve Weintraub. As the book took shape, the voice and influence of my first Buddhist teacher, Shunryu Suzuki Roshi, emerged more and more strongly. Though he died many years ago, his teachings live on and continue to grow. Thanks also to my chorus of encouragers: Lama Surya Das, Jack Kornfield, Seymour and Sylvia Boorstein, and most of all my wife, Amy, my first reader and life love.

My agent, Eileen Cope, helped me imagine this book nearly four years ago. Through major illness and many detours, her nourishment and support has been invaluable.

And finally, a book this complex and multilayered needs the sure touch of a gifted editor, and I have certainly had one in Tracy Behar. From the first, she understood what I was trying to say, and found so many ways to help me say it better.

BIBLIOGRAPHY

Brown, Edward Espe. *Tomato Blessings and Radish Teachings*. New York: Riverhead Books, 1997.

Bulow, Louis, ed. "Kolbe, Saint of Auschwitz." www.auschwitz. dk/kolbe.htm, 2001–2003.

Chadwick, David. *Crooked Cucumber*. New York: Broadway Books, 2001.

Conze, Edward. *Buddhism: Its Essence and Development*. New York: Harper & Row, 1975.

———. *Buddhist Thought in India*. Ann Arbor, MI: The University of Michigan Press, 1982.

Erikson, Erik. *Childhood and Society*. New York: W.W. Norton & Company, 1993.

Fountain, Henry. "When Backyards Were Laboratories." *New York Times,* May 19, 2002.

Graham, Dom Aelred. *Conversations: Christian and Buddhist*. New York: Harcourt, Brace & World, Inc., 1968.

Guenther, H. V. *The Jewel Ornament of Liberation*. Berkeley, CA: Shambala Publications, Inc., 1971.

Hopkins, Jeffrey, Ph.D. *Cultivating Compassion*. New York: Broadway Books, 2001.

Masson, Jeffrey. *Dogs Never Lie About Love*. New York: Crown Publishers, 1997.

Mitchell, Robert Allen. *The Buddha: His Life Retold*. New York: Paragon House, 1989.

Quindlen, Anna. "Doing Nothing Is Something." *Newsweek,* May 13, 2002.

Snyder, Gary. *The Real Work: Interviews & Talks, 1964–1979*. New York: New Directions Publishing, 1980.

Stevens, John. *One Robe, One Bowl: The Zen Poetry of Ryokan*. New York: Weatherhill, 1977.

Suzuki, Shunryu. *Branching Streams Flow in the Darkness*. Berkeley and Los Angeles: Universiy of California Press, 1999.

———. *Not Always So*. New York: HarperCollins, 2002.

———. *Zen Mind, Beginner's Mind*. New York: Walker/Weatherhill, 1970.

Tucker, Robert C., ed. *The Marx-Engels Reader,* second edition. New York: W.W. Norton & Company, 1978.

Welch, Lew. *Ring of Bone: Collected Poems, 1950–1971*. Bolinas, CA: Grey Fox Press, 1979.

Wilson Ross, Nancy. *Buddhism: A Way of Life and Thought*. New York: Alfred A. Knopf, 1981.

Yuasa, Nobuyuki, tr. *The Zen Poems of Ryokan*. Princeton, NJ: Princeton University Press, 1981.

INDEX

Index

Index

Index